What Leaders Are Saying …

I had the privilege of attending the WILD training offered by Gateway Women. At that point in my ministry, I was discouraged and disheartened about my assignment as a Senior Pastor's wife and leader of our Women's Ministry. In each session I attended, the teachings spoke healing to my soul, equipped me with the tools to be a more effective and confident leader, and inspired me to embrace my assignment. I am grateful for WILD and how greatly it impacted my life. I continue to use the teachings to train and equip women leaders in my local church.

Pastor Tonya McGill
Executive Pastor/Women's Ministry Leader
Antioch Christian Church, Irving, Texas

The Bible instructs us to equip the saints to do the work of the ministry. When my campus began to grow quickly, I needed a way to develop high-level leaders while getting to know them on a relational level. The unique combination of spiritual and practical teaching, along with personal activation, is what makes WILD effective and special. It allows women to hear God, understand who He created and called them to be, and express their discoveries in a safe environment. WILD allows me to get to know ministry leaders in a small environment where I can hear their passions and watch them be transformed. WILD will take your women and your ministry to the next level. It is worth your time and investment.

Adana Wilson
Pastor, Adult Ministries
Gateway Church, Frisco, Texas

My first experience with WILD was as an uninformed participant. I had no idea what to expect. The experience awakened me to the simplicity of receiving from God—His love, His methods, and His purpose for my life.

Now as a WILD ministry leader, I have been delighted to see my personal passion come to life as professional women are empowered by their faith in the workplace. I have watched women awaken to the simplicity of hearing God and embrace His love, methods, and purpose for their lives. You will see this curriculum open hearts and lead to the same healing and empowerment for the women you lead. What a joy to see so much hidden talent come alive! It's my favorite thing.

Mari Eisenrich
CEO
Weatherby-Eisenrich Insurance, Southlake, Texas

Women in Leadership Development (WILD) is about more than just leadership; it's also about community, encouragement, and relationship with our Savior. For me as a pastor, WILD has been the greatest tool to get to know and hear the hearts of the women God has put in our campus. The curriculum encourages and challenges women to dig deeper and to go to places that sometimes we don't allow ourselves to enter. I have seen women come alive to their destinies and begin the journey toward their callings.

Lorena Valle
Pastor, Adult Ministries
Gateway Church, North Richland Hills, Texas

WILD allows women of all ages to experience nurture, guidance, and release in their calls to servant leadership. The nurture, guidance, and release I was blessed to receive during my fellowship year with the Barbara Bush Foundation was instrumental in all God has done, and continues to do, in my sphere of education. Every woman who senses God's call to serve should experience the God-breath that is resident in each of the wonderful women in this life-changing program.

Dr. Feyi Obamehinti
Managing Director
Ravir LLC, Keller, Texas

As a WILD leader, I have a front row seat to watch women's eyes being opened as their passions, dreams, and God-given direction turn into tangible paths for them to pursue. My favorite thing is when a woman says to me, "I had no idea my life was going to be changed so much in just a few short sessions." It is the presence of God that brings this rapid transformation. I love being invited to watch, lead, and cheer for them all.

Marsia Van Wormer
Associate Pastor, Community Outreach
Gateway Church, Southlake, Texas

What Participants Are Saying ...

WILD has been my graduate-level preparation for life and godliness. After 14 years at home, it launched me into the marketplace and deposited me in a position where my strengths are used daily, my passions are well-satisfied, and God's purposes are being fulfilled in and through me. I'm living in my sweet spot because of WILD.

Sheila Shupp

WILD has been an incredible learning journey for me. It is a safe place to hone and grow your skills and confidence. I am so thankful that I was included in this community of strong, encouraging, and zesty women who all have unique expressions of the same heart: we love Jesus.

Lauren Dunn

WILD is a journey to unlock the gifting and calling God has for your life. I can pinpoint the time in my life when my eyes were opened to see myself as God sees me. The process began when I said *yes* to WILD, and I am so thankful that I did.

Lisa Corley

WILD is wonderful—new friends, great teachings, challenging assignments, and the personal growth that comes from all these experiences. But what made the greatest impact on me is what Pastor Lynda Grove said at the first WILD class I attended. She asked, "What is our motivation for leadership?" It was a reminder and a challenge to each of us that what we do, on or off a platform, is not for our own gain. Everything we do is for God's glory.

Judy Brisky

I love how WILD created a forever sisterhood! The Lord made it clear that the WILD journey had only just begun.

Lucy Wallace

Leader Guide

WILD

Leader Guide

WOMEN IN LEADERSHIP DEVELOPMENT

FROM GATEWAY WOMEN
FOREWORD BY DEBBIE MORRIS

Leader Guide

WILD Women in Leadership Development: Leader Guide
Copyright © 2018 by Gateway Women

Unless otherwise noted, Scripture taken from the New King James Version®. Copyright © 1982 by Thomas Nelson. Used by permission. All rights reserved.

Scripture quotations taken from the Amplified® Bible (AMPC), Copyright © 1954, 1958, 1962, 1964, 1965, 1987 by The Lockman Foundation. Used by permission. www.Lockman.org.

Scripture quotations are from the ESV® Bible (The Holy Bible, English Standard Version®), copyright © 2001 by Crossway, a publishing ministry of Good News Publishers. Used by permission. All rights reserved.

Scripture quotations taken from the New American Standard Bible® (NASB), Copyright © 1960, 1962, 1963, 1968, 1971, 1972, 1973, 1975, 1977, 1995 by The Lockman Foundation. Used by permission. www.Lockman.org.

Scripture quotations marked (NIV) are taken from the Holy Bible, New International Version®, NIV®. Copyright © 1973, 1978, 1984, 2011 by Biblica, Inc.™ Used by permission of Zondervan. All rights reserved worldwide. www.zondervan.com. The "NIV" and "New International Version" are trademarks registered in the United States Patent and Trademark Office by Biblica, Inc.

Scripture quotations marked (NLT) are taken from the Holy Bible, New Living Translation, copyright ©1996, 2004, 2007, 2013, 2015 by Tyndale House Foundation. Used by permission of Tyndale House Publishers, Inc., Carol Stream, Illinois 60188. All rights reserved.

The Promise Principle Journal by Phillip Hunter: Copyright © 2017 Gateway Press. All rights reserved. Used by permission.

Promise Principle™ and the *PP*™ logo are registered trademarks of Gateway Publishing.

All rights reserved. No portion of this publication may be reproduced, stored in a retrieval system, or transmitted in any form by any means—electronic, mechanical, photocopying, recording, or any other—without prior permission from the publisher.

ISBN: 978-1-945529-45-0 Paperback

We hope you hear from the Holy Spirit and receive God's richest blessings from this book by Gateway Press. We want to provide the highest quality resources that take the messages, music, and media of Gateway Church to the world. For more information on other resources from Gateway Publishing, go to gatewaypublishing.com.

Gateway Press, an imprint of Gateway Publishing
700 Blessed Way
Southlake, Texas 76092
gatewaypublishing.com

18 19 20 21 22 5 4 3 2 1
Printed in the United States of America

This book is dedicated to the women of Gateway Church.
You are beautiful leaders.
Thank you for the privilege of watching you grow in your gifts.
You make us all better, stronger, and more effective.

Table of Contents

Foreword xiii
Acknowledgments xv
Getting Ready for WILD xvii

    Why WILD? xix
    Getting Familiar xxi
    Getting Started xxiii
    Sample Email Invitation xxv
    Sample Email for Participant Confirmation xxvi
    Evaluation Instructions xxvii
    Sample Evaluation xxviii
    Recommended Agendas xxix
    Dear Leader of Women xxxvii

Welcome to WILD 1
Session 1 3
Session 2 25
Session 3 49
Session 4 67
Session 5 89
Session 6 107
Session 7 119

Until We Meet Again 133
About Gateway Women 135
About Pink Impact 136
Additional Gateway Women Resources 137

Foreword

When we first pioneered Gateway Church, the Lord called me to Women's Ministry. I rose to the challenge, reluctantly at first, feeling more drafted than invited. But as I learned to lean into my position and not resist it, I found abundant grace and soon realized the calling suited me.

My heart became burdened for the preparation of the next generation of women as leaders and influencers. By this time, our women's ministry was well underway, yet I sensed there was more we could do to invest in Gateway Church's women. While hosting a leadership roundtable, the concept of a special development class for women leaders was proposed. Debbie Stuart, former Director of Women's Ministry at Prestonwood Baptist Church, shared her leadership development concept called WILD.

I was with Lynda Grove at the time, and we loved what we heard. We were eager to construct a curriculum that instilled leadership principles into the women of Gateway Church. We knew we needed to prepare women intentionally as leaders, and we desired to accomplish this through relationship. Debbie Stuart graciously gave us permission to use the WILD title, and we spent the next several months crafting the curriculum for our own WILD ministry. We launched that first class with expectant hearts.

Since then, the women's leadership team has been on an exciting journey. Through the relational training of WILD, we dedicate ourselves to helping Gateway Church's women rise to their fullest potential. We intentionally keep WILD classes small to create an atmosphere that allows enduring bonds of friendship between the staff and our women, as well as among the women themselves.

Although completing the class does not guarantee a leadership position, it has propelled many women into the next stage of their destinies. Some have started ministries, businesses, and magazines. Others have written books and taken leadership roles with great purpose and confidence, both inside and outside the church. The testimonies from the women of WILD are so inspiring. I love what Lauren Dunn says of her time in WILD: "It provides a safe place to step into your own skin." And Sheila Shupp says, "WILD is my kind of fun! It's like positioning yourself under a great mother's purposeful training. In WILD, I finally grasped how perfectly I am made. I learned how my strengths work together and how to use them for kingdom purposes."

As leaders, it is crucial for us to grasp the potential of our influence to empower the next generation. WILD provides a great opportunity to equip women to lead with excellence. We are excited to share our vision with you, and we are thankful for your willingness to impact the women in your church.

Debbie Morris
Executive Pastor, Gateway Women
Gateway Church

Acknowledgments

We are better together!

From its strategy to its content, from the initial dream to the present reality, WILD was developed in an atmosphere of relationship and designed to be implemented the same way. Because of such focus on relationship, many people were involved in the birth and development of this training.

Thank you, Pastor Mallory Bassham, Dr. Cassie Reid, and the Gateway Women's leadership team, for your contributions to the development of the content and teaching of WILD. You have helped shape the heart and message of this ministry. Many graduates have been forever impacted by your love and service.

Thank you, Dana Stone, for compiling the first Leader Guide and for bravely taking a variety of teachings, activations, and ideas and turning them into something wonderful. You took vision and brought it to life. There wouldn't be anything to share with others without you and your gifts.

Thank you, Jen de LaPorte and Christy Linder, for helping us develop the Participant Journal and for assisting us in taking this manuscript across the finish line.

Thank you, Pastor Phillip Hunter, for developing the Bible study technique, the *Promise Principle*™, and thank you, Gateway Church, for allowing us to use excerpts from *The Promise Principle Journal*.

Over the years several key lay leaders have served the women of Gateway Church through WILD. Thank you, Penny Spurling, Lisa Corley, and Mari Eisenrich, for your selfless devotion to the gifts and callings of others. You've all been role models of godly leadership.

Of course, WILD wouldn't even exist without the vision and oversight of Pastor Debbie Morris. Pastor Debbie was the first to say that we have to find a way to identify and develop more women leaders. She's always been the champion of others, and WILD has been a way for her to make her personal passion come to life. Thank you, Pastor Debbie, for leading the way for all of us.

Thank you, Gateway Publishing, for taking these valuable teachings and shaping them into a curriculum for churches around the world. Craig Dunnagan, John Andersen, Kathy Krenzien, James Reid, Jenny Morgan, Peyton Sepeda, and Caleb Jobe all worked to make this a successful project.

Finally, we want to express our personal appreciation to the women of Gateway Church who have graciously allowed us to field test this material for years. Your beautiful faces and your amazing gifts have inspired us. You are treasures to the body of Christ, and we are so proud of you for honoring God with every ounce of your passion and leadership calling.

GETTING READY FOR WILD

Why WILD?

In today's busy world it's difficult to get to know all the women in your church on a personal level. It's hard to scan your Sunday morning service and know anything significant about every woman you see. Even if you spot some women with leadership potential, it's difficult to entrust them with assignments if you don't know anything about their spiritual journeys. How can you identify, develop, and release women more effectively into leadership roles? How can you share your core values and shape the growth of these women in a way that produces healthy fruit? How can you share the workload or expand your ministry outreach without more qualified and prepared leaders?

These very questions led us to develop a plan of action for investing in emerging leaders. WILD (Women in Leadership Development) was born out of a desire for a relationship with the women in our church. As Gateway Church grew, it became increasingly difficult to form personal relationships with potential leaders and release them to use their gifts for ministry. We found ourselves reaching the edge of our ministry limits because we could not see or invest in women outside our immediate circle of relationships.

We set out to create a tool to engage women face-to-face in a small group setting over several sessions. We hoped to gain both relationships and insight into their personal passions and callings. We realized the ability to build relationships was an important first step in finding and establishing leaders we could trust.

When we started WILD, we had no idea how popular this training would become or how it would create such strong bonds among the participants. Not only did we get to know them, but they also got to know us and one another. Relationships have been the greatest benefit by far. The sense of belonging and purpose that came to these women is what really propelled them further into their destinies.

But relationships were not the only benefit. Each woman also experienced a personal journey of self-discovery. Through a simple format of teaching, hearing God, and activating exercises, the Holy Spirit began to move in each woman's heart in miraculous ways. The primary goal of the training is not to get a leadership assignment. It's not about being a platform speaker or small group leader. The goal is for the women to press into God to know themselves more thoroughly and to agree with Him about what makes each of them unique and special.

Over the years we've watched God develop these women in a variety of ways. Some went on to embrace a season at home with grace and confidence. Others started businesses or ministries. Some wrote books. Some became health experts. Many began to volunteer within the walls of our church as they followed their personal interests and passions. These women have become a sort of sisterhood, recognizing that the process of WILD releases a sense of belonging and appreciation for one another.

WILD received so much positive feedback that leaders from other churches started asking us for information. The curriculum you are about to explore was designed by a team of female leaders who are passionate about developing women for godly purposes. It is our honor to share with you the tools, teachings, and vision we have successfully used to draw out the best in others. Here you will find a simple overview and outline of the strategies we use to awaken revelation and deposit truth in our own leaders.

We offer this curriculum as a guide to our recommended best practices. Take time to customize the topics and exercises to reflect your church's core values and mission statement. We include some pre-work items to help you get started. All along the way, we give insight and encouragement to help you maximize each session's content. You aren't alone on this journey—we are right there with you!

So prepare yourself to be blown away by the beauty and grace of the women God has placed all around you. We believe you are about to be blessed with a multitude of new friends, ready leaders, and exciting ministry opportunities.

Getting Familiar

Leader Guide

We want to help you make the most of this Leader Guide. Our goal is to minimize your need for preparation and maximize your impact. We've included several things to assist you with each session:

- **Leader Coaching Notes** provide helpful information regarding the format, purpose, and application of specific sections.
- **Leader Instructions** aid in administering the teachings, activations, and homework assignments.
- **Recommended Agendas** give a sample schedule for each session.
- **Teachings** include detailed notes but can also be modified to fit the needs/interests of each class.
- **Activations** give participants opportunities to engage and provide feedback throughout the sessions. These exercises are designed to help the women gain confidence in their capacity to hear God, know His love for them, and grow in their ability to communicate spiritual truths with clarity and excellence.

Participant Journal

The Participant Journal is a companion to the Leader Guide and includes a general outline of the teachings and space to take notes. It also has a place to document homework assignments or things the women hear from God. We encourage you to keep a copy of the Participant Journal for your own review and use. We find it helpful to remind ourselves about the contents of the Participant Journal before each session so we can maximize these tools and help the women document their experiences.

The following aspects of the Participant Journal are also included in the Leader Guide for your convenience:

- **Participant Instructions**: Leaders should review these instructions prior to each session and be prepared to answer any questions. The page number on which the instructions are listed in the Participant Journal is included in the Leader Guide.
- **Character Builder**: Each session includes one value that emphasizes the importance of God's Word and the development of character as part of the women's WILD experience. You can incorporate the value into your meeting time as you see fit.
- **Homework**: These assignments are completed outside of class and submitted at the following session. For Session 6, leaders are encouraged to develop their own assignment.
- **Personal Reflection**: These thought-provoking questions prepare the participants' hearts for the content of the upcoming session. They are designed to open a dialogue between the women and God. You may find the questions helpful as introductions for your teachings each session.
- **The *Promise Principle***: This study is optional but very valuable. We want to encourage the women to spend time in the Word of God so they can understand and apply God's principles. You may want to build feedback or sharing around this exercise into your agenda. For further study, *The Promise Principle* and *The Promise Principle Journal* can be purchased separately from Gateway Press. Additional information can be found at the end of this Leader Guide.

Ongoing Community

We recommend encouraging participants to further develop their leadership calling and relationships by continuing to meet with each other following the WILD class. We invite the women at Gateway Church to form small groups and use the book *Integrity: The Courage to Meet the Demands of Reality* by Dr. Henry Cloud. This resource is an additional expense which you will want to evaluate and consider before the final session of the class.

Getting Started

You have decided to host a WILD class. Great! To get started you need to:
- **Determine the details**. Begin by setting the date, location, and maximum number of participants you want to include in this class.
- **Invite a few trusted women to help you lead WILD**. Our team usually consists of three designated leaders. In addition, we often invite guest speakers to teach the content when it pertains to an area they have mastered. For example, we often ask one of our pastors who is an excellent writer to teach the class on writing skills. You will notice that each session contains teaching times and one or more activations. We have found that sharing these moments across a team of leaders is most effective.
- **Pray and carefully select your initial class**. Over the years we have said WILD is by invitation only but is not exclusive. We maintain a list of women who have a desire to participate or who we believe would benefit from the experience. When it's time to offer a class, we send an email invitation. We limit the size of classes, so we typically accept participants on a first come, first served basis. However, when we began WILD, every participant was hand-selected. We began with women we knew and could identify as leaders. Many of them had been serving with us for quite some time. This method gave us the grace to test our content and discover what we didn't even know about the ladies with whom we were doing life. Once word gets out—and it will—you can take recommendations from prior participants and even allow women you don't know (but who desire to grow as leaders) to participate. Soon you will want to form a waiting list for the class. You are going to be so excited to discover the treasures within your own church!

- **Email to confirm participation.** Contact the women you have selected for participation in the class and give them all the details needed to prepare.
- **Use support documents.** We have included a sample email invitation, a sample email for participation confirmation, and a sample evaluation form for feedback at the end of your class. We've also included a *Recommended Agenda* for each session. We developed two timelines for you to consider, based on the size of the class. The larger the gathering, the more time you will need. We have offered class lengths of 75 minutes and 120 minutes. Remember—we offer these agendas based on our best practices. You should customize them to fit your needs.
- **WILD Participant Journal.** We highly recommend that every woman in the class uses the WILD Participant Journal. Participants greatly benefit from it as a place to record their experiences. The Participant Journal follows the format of the Leader Guide and makes it easy for each woman to document what she is learning and hearing from God.

Sample Email Invitation

Dear (name of potential participant),

We are excited to invite you to a special leadership development class for women. We are inviting you because you have been identified as an emerging leader, and we want to invest in your personal development. This class, called WILD (Women in Leadership Development), is designed to help you deepen your relationship with the Holy Spirit and challenge you to take action on the things He has placed within you.

WILD is a seven-session commitment. Each session will meet on _____ (day of the week) at _____ (time of day) for _____ (length of time). (Or give the scheduled dates and times if it is a unique schedule.) During this time, you will have an opportunity to meet new friends and hear specific teachings on topics related to healthy leadership. You will be asked at various times to participate in class activities and do outside homework. You will even be given opportunities for additional journal and study time.

Please mark your calendar now for the following dates:
(Include your schedule here.)

Since participation in WILD is by invitation only, please respond by _____ (include a deadline). If you are unable to take part in a WILD class at this time, please respond and let us know if you would like us to consider you for a future class.

Thank you in advance for considering this invitation.

Blessings,

(Your name and contact information)

Sample Email for Participant Confirmation

Dear (name of selected participant),

Welcome to WILD (Women in Leadership Development)!

We are so excited for you to join us in this incredible leadership experience. This class is designed to allow you to meet with the Holy Spirit and challenge you to take action on the things He has placed within you.

WILD is a seven-session commitment (or another number, if applicable).

Our first class will meet on _____ (date) at _____ (time) at _____ (location). The remainder of the schedule is as follows:

(Include all meeting dates for the class and any information needed to help plan her participation.)

Please come prepared with an open heart, a willingness to reach outside your comfort zone, and a sense of anticipation.

Let us know if you have any questions!

Blessings,

(Your name and contact information)

Evaluation Instructions

We highly encourage WILD participants to complete and return an evaluation of the class during the final session. Evaluations help us build upon and improve each WILD experience. We have provided a sample form on the following page. You are welcome to make photocopies of this form, or you may use the questions as a guide and create your own form.

WOMEN IN LEADERSHIP DEVELOPMENT
EVALUATION

1. Did this class meet your expectations? Why or why not?

   _____
   _____

2. Describe one thing you will take away from this class.

   _____
   _____

3. What other topics or leadership subjects would have been beneficial to you?

   _____
   _____

4. Would you recommend this class to a friend? If so, please give us her name and contact information.

   _____
   _____

5. Please add any additional information you would like us to know.

   _____
   _____

Recommended Agendas

Recommended agendas are included as sample schedules for each session. These recommendations reflect our best practices. However, *you can alter them to fit almost any platform or group size.* This curriculum is adaptable to different needs.

For example, one of our favorite classes occurred in the summer and included a group of "20-somethings." The group met on Monday, Tuesday, and Thursday evenings for two weeks. The experience was powerful. We've also modified the agenda and format for a two-day retreat with over 100 participants. At another time, we adjusted the agenda for a working women's group that met every third Sunday morning to accommodate busy schedules.

For each session, we include two schedules, based on the number of participants in the class. If you have 8 to 10 women, then you will need at least one hour and fifteen minutes. If you have 11 to 20 women, you will probably need as much as two hours or more.

Session 1 Agenda

Character Builder: Humility

Help the women get to know each other and become comfortable with the dynamics of WILD. You will also introduce them to the importance of hearing God. They will then use the Participant Journal to understand, record, and retain the full scope of what He is saying.

	8–10 Participants *(75 Minutes)*	11–20 Participants *(120 Minutes)*
Welcome/Greet/Prayer	5 minutes	5 minutes
Teaching 1: The Vision and Purpose of WILD	20 minutes	20 minutes
Activation: Getting to Know One Another	30 minutes	60 minutes
Teaching 2: Overview of WILD	15 minutes	30 minutes
Homework Explanation & Closing Prayer	5 minutes	5 minutes

Session 2 Agenda

Character Builder: Integrity

Impart the DNA for leadership and encourage the women to embrace an identity based on how God sees them. Inspire and challenge them to hear Him, believe what He says, and obey His voice. Help them understand how their security and confidence are found in knowing God.

	8–10 Participants *(75 Minutes)*	**11–20 Participants** *(120 Minutes)*
Welcome/Greet/Prayer	5 minutes	5 minutes
Teaching 1: Identity in Christ	20 minutes	35 minutes
Activation: Who Do You Say I Am?	20 minutes	35 minutes
Teaching 2: Core Values & Qualities of Effective Leaders	20 minutes	35 minutes
Homework Explanation: Project Development	5 minutes	5 minutes
Closing Prayer	5 minutes	5 minutes

Session 3 Agenda

Character Builder: Service

Inspire the women to pursue true heart transformations in which they will learn to serve others and silence the voice of comparison. As a woman discovers her real identity, she can embrace the truth that her unique gifts are a tool to help her fulfill the unique plan God has for her life.

	8–10 Participants *(75 Minutes)*	**11–20 Participants** *(120 Minutes)*
Welcome/Greet/Prayer	5 minutes	5 minutes
Teaching 1: Finding Your Passion	20 minutes	30 minutes
Activation: Share the Gifts You See in Others	20 minutes	40 minutes
Teaching 2: Comparison	20 minutes	30 minutes
Activation: Breaking Comparison & Affirming Identity in Christ	5 minutes	10 minutes
Homework Explanation & Closing Prayer	5 minutes	5 minutes

Session 4 Agenda

Character Builder: Excellence
God calls each of us to give testimony to the things He has done. Encourage the women to find their voices and remove any distractions. They will learn to conquer nervousness, fear, and negative body language.

	8–10 Participants *(75 Minutes)*	11–20 Participants *(120 Minutes)*
Welcome/Greet/Prayer	5 minutes	5 minutes
Activation: Passion Presentations	25 minutes	60 minutes
Teaching 1: Speaking Tips	15 minutes	20 minutes
Activation: Practice Speaking Skills	5 minutes	5 minutes
Teaching 2: Writing Tips	20 minutes	25 minutes
Homework Explanation & Closing Prayer	5 minutes	5 minutes

Session 5 Agenda

Character Builder: Unity

The most beautiful evidence of a Spirit-led leader is the fruit of the Spirit in her life. We should all encourage and love one another.

	8–10 Participants *(75 Minutes)*	11–20 Participants *(120 Minutes)*
Welcome/Greet/Prayer	5 minutes	5 minutes
Teaching: Spirit-Led Leaders	20 minutes	20 minutes
Activation: Share Your Blog or Devotional	30 minutes	65 minutes
Activation: Words of Encouragement	15 minutes	25 minutes
Homework Explanation & Closing Prayer	5 minutes	5 minutes

Session 6 Agenda

Character Builder: Christlikeness

Spiritual maturity is the goal of every believer. The more we understand the character and nature of God, the more we will reflect His love for people.

	8–10 Participants *(75 Minutes)*	**11–20 Participants** *(120 Minutes)*
Welcome/Greet/Prayer	5 minutes	5 minutes
Activation: Project Presentations	65 minutes	110 minutes
Homework Explanation & Closing Prayer	5 minutes	5 minutes

Session 7 Agenda

Character Builder: Submission
Understanding the importance, power, and protection of mutual submission to one another is a critical sign of spiritual growth.

	8–10 Participants (75 Minutes)	11–20 Participants (120 Minutes)
Welcome/Greet/Prayer	5 minutes	5 minutes
Teaching: Embracing What's Next	20 minutes	30 minutes
Activation: Ongoing Community	35 minutes	70 minutes
Activation: Celebration	5 minutes	5 minutes
Evaluation Forms	5 minutes	5 minutes
Closing Prayer & Blessing	5 minutes	5 minutes

Dear Leader of Women

I don't think of myself as a video gamer, but I've played my fair share of them.

When I sit down to play, I begin by selecting a character pre-programmed with unique abilities, weapons, or tools. However, whether I'm looking at Mario at the starting line in his signature Kart or a camo-clad, AK-toting Ranger, my chosen character is limited—useless even—until I take hold of the controller and strategically aim to win. My character will never win the race, conquer the enemy, or advance to the next level if I do nothing. The same is true of the women I lead. If I want to see these women discover their passions and reach their fullest potential, then I must take hold of the adventure before me and not wait for their spiritual growth to "happen" spontaneously.

In the book of Judges, Gideon leads the nation of Israel to victory over its enemies. However, he doesn't understand his leadership potential until God calls him to fight. Gideon becomes a national hero, but when the fighting is over, he simply returns home. The land has peace for 40 years, but as soon as Gideon dies, Israel returns to its idols and rejects the Lord (Judges 8:33). What a tragic ending to an exciting adventure! It makes me wonder if Gideon ever fully grasped the potential of the influence he carried. Although he was personally victorious, would his influence have been longer-lasting if he had developed other leaders?

At the beginning of my own leadership adventure, I didn't even realize I was a leader until Pastor Debbie Morris saw potential in me. She taught me how to discover the exciting plans God has for me. As we developed WILD together, I found my own leadership gifts released and used in ways I had never dreamed. I pray the same will be true for you.

God is WILD about us. He invites each one of us to an exciting adventure. You are embarking on a journey to help the women in your church discover the leader within—the potential hidden in the form of their gifts, talents, and passions. While we are each called to a unique adventure, every one of us is called, first and foremost, to God Himself. Knowing God, hearing His voice, believing Him, and obeying Him are the keys to taking hold of the impossible and championing others on their adventures. I encourage you to emphasize and teach these significant keys throughout this training so your participants will become more like Christ. On this WILD journey, you will discover all things are possible. You will become the champion who helps others do the same.

Lynda Grove
Pastor of Women
Gateway Church

WELCOME TO WILD

session 1

TO EVERYTHING THERE IS A SEASON,
and a time for every matter or purpose under heaven...
HE HAS MADE EVERYTHING BEAUTIFUL IN ITS TIME.
He also has planted eternity in men's hearts and minds
(A DIVINELY IMPLANTED SENSE OF A PURPOSE
working through the ages which nothing under the sun but
GOD ALONE CAN SATISFY),
yet so that men cannot find out what GOD HAS DONE
FROM THE BEGINNING *to the* END...
I KNOW THAT WHATEVER GOD DOES,
IT ENDURES FOREVER;
nothing can be added to it NOR ANYTHING TAKEN FROM IT.
And God does it so that men will (reverently) fear Him, (revere and worship Him,
KNOWING THAT HE IS).
ECCLESIASTES 3:1, 11, 14 (AMPC)

Session 1

· · · • · · ·
Leader Coaching Note
Each session begins with a Character Builder featured in both the Leader Guide and the Participant Journal. Briefly discuss this topic as part of the session's welcome, recap, and introduction. You can add more emphasis to this area if you desire.

In Session 1, you will help the women get to know each other and become comfortable with the dynamics of WILD. You will also introduce them to the importance of hearing God. They will then use the Participant Journal to understand, record, and retain the full scope of what He is saying.
· · · • · · ·

Agenda

	8–10 Participants (75 Minutes)	11–20 Participants (120 Minutes)
Welcome/Greet/Prayer	5 minutes	5 minutes
Teaching 1: The Vision and Purpose of WILD	20 minutes	20 minutes
Activation: Getting to Know One Another	30 minutes	60 minutes
Teaching 2: Overview of WILD	15 minutes	30 minutes
Homework Explanation & Closing Prayer	5 minutes	5 minutes

Character Builder
HUMILITY

Page 5 in the Participant Journal

Definition

- Being free from pride or arrogance
- Thinking of others above yourself (Romans 12:3; Proverbs 3:34)

Reading

Acts 11–15

Biblical Application

Barnabas was sent by the Jerusalem church to see what was happening in the church at Antioch. Then he went to Tarsus to seek Saul (later Paul). Barnabas paved the way for Paul's ministry. We see him first seeking Paul (Acts 11:25), then ministering alongside him (Acts 12–15), and then they go separate ways (Acts 15:38–39). Barnabas was not intimidated when asked to help someone else rise in leadership; he was happy to play his unique role.

Personal Application

- How often do you find yourself falsely discrediting your strengths, gifts, or accomplishments to gain more recognition?
- How do you respond when you receive compliments that acknowledge your gifts or a job you have done well?
- How do you respond when the credit or reward you deserve is overlooked or given to another person?

SESSION 1

Teaching 1: The Vision and Purpose of WILD

Page 9 in the Participant Journal

· • · • ● • · • ·

Leader Coaching Note

This first WILD teaching begins with an emphasis on setting healthy expectations. The women most likely came to your group with excitement.
At the same time, they don't know exactly what to expect. You can help them by exploring their expectations to see if there are things God has already begun to stir in their hearts. You will be able to connect with them as a leader by learning about these expectations.

· • · • ● • · • ·

Leader Instructions

As you prepare to teach, put yourself in the place of the women who will be attending your class. What questions will they bring with them? What is causing them anxiety? You will find answers to the most common questions in this teaching. Add anything else you feel will be helpful for the women.

You can open the discussion by saying, "If I were you, I would probably be asking myself ..." Then share some of the questions and answers you discovered as you thought about the women in your class. Encourage the participants to ask as many questions as they'd like. This will help you establish trust and calm any fears they may have.

1. Why Are You Here?
You are here because:

- We recognize and value the gift of leadership we see in you.
- We believe you have a calling and purpose on your life, and we would like to help you prepare to walk in it fully.
- There is a time and place for everything. Your time to dig into the things of God is *now*! This is *your season—your opportunity—*to receive an impartation from the Lord.

2. What Is the Vision of WILD?
The vision of WILD is to help you:

- Grow in the gifts and callings God has on your life
- Draw out the goodness of the Lord in your heart
- Stand with you as this goodness is revealed
- Build women of strength, service, and courage in this generation

· • · · ● · • · ·

Leader Coaching Note

Some women mistakenly believe that participating in WILD automatically ensures a leadership position for them to step into and begin using their newfound confidence and calling. Now is the time to clarify what you are offering through WILD. Encourage the women by telling them God's plan and timing are always best. The primary goal is not to put them in just any leadership role that needs filling but to encourage them to seek God for a perfect fit. It is incredible to watch God open doors for each woman.

· • · ● · • · ·

3. What Is the Purpose of WILD?
The purpose of WILD is to help you:

- Become established on a strong spiritual foundation
- Hear the Holy Spirit and act on His direction
- Prepare to lead and influence others to do the same
- Identify leadership strengths
- Become empowered to use your gifts and walk in your calling and purpose—God's will for your life for the glory of His kingdom

Leader Instructions

(As you move into Point 4 of this teaching, you might find it helpful to use the following exercise.)

Prepare a whiteboard, large wall sticky note, or flip chart to make a list. Write the word "Expectations" in large letters at the top.

Then say to the women, "Many of you came wondering what this class is about. Some of you may have an idea, but all of you came expectantly. What are some expectations you have for this class?"

Listen and begin to write as the women share their expectations.

Positively affirm each person's response. This is a time for them to engage. Respond with encouraging words, such as "Good," "Great," "OK," or "What else?" The purpose is to foster open communication; no correction is necessary at this point.

4. What Can I Expect?
You can expect:

- To hear the Lord more clearly about His purpose and calling for you
- To identify, communicate, and grow in the gifts and strengths the Lord has placed inside you
- To develop friendships
- To step into your calling more fully and intentionally so you can effectively make a difference in the world

Activation: Getting to Know One Another

Page 13 in the Participant Journal

• • • • • • •

Leader Coaching Note
This is the first time the women will stand in front of the class and share something personal. Many of them will be nervous. Help them feel relaxed and comfortable. Your goal is to reduce anxiety and help everyone focus on the things you want to celebrate as a group. Set an expectation of vulnerability, emphasize the importance of personal connection, and encourage the women to get to know each other.

• • • • • • •

Leader Instructions

Use this opportunity to activate the hearts of the women in your class. Begin by having them introduce themselves to their classmates. (Depending on the size of your class, you can have the women introduce themselves by name only or offer additional details. If you have a particularly large class, you may wish to divide the women into groups.)

Once everyone has met, tell the women to turn to page 13 in the Participant Journal. Read the Participant Instructions (see below) out loud. After the women write down their answers, ask for a volunteer to be the first to share her answers. Applaud each person as she completes the exercise.

Participant Instructions

Take two minutes to think about and write down your answers to the following questions. Then be prepared to share your answers with the class.

1. **What brought me here?**
2. **What do I expect to gain from this class?**

SESSION 1

Teaching 2: Overview of WILD

Page 14 in the Participant Journal

· · · • · · ·

Leader Coaching Note
After you have gone through the Introduction to WILD, you will give the women a more thorough explanation of what they will be doing and the materials they will be using. You will also help them understand how to use the Participant Journal and introduce them to the Promise Principle™.

· · · • · · ·

All in the Mindset

The women will find themselves stretched during every session of this class. As the leader, you will challenge them to remain vulnerable and open to where the Lord is taking them. Encourage them to allow God to unlock things within them, go places they have shut off, or do things they thought were impossible. Allow their relationships to build here. In previous classes, these relationships have led to lifelong friendships, accountability/prayer partners, and small groups. This is a journey! Encourage the women to commit to the process and to dig into the homework and activations. This is how they will get the most out of the class.

· · · • · · ·

Leader Coaching Note
Over the years we have seen women struggle to keep all their notes, activations, homework, and words from God in one place. For this reason, we created the Participant Journal. In addition to being an organizational tool, the Participant

Journal serves as a place for the women to create an ongoing dialogue with God while they develop a deeper love for His Word. Don't assume talking with God is a natural experience for all your participants or that they are already comfortable with this kind of terminology. As they move through the class, they will learn to become more intimate with the Holy Spirit and easily converse with Him. In future sessions, they will have specific homework assignments to complete and share. In each session, you will see Personal Reflection and the Promise Principle included as optional activities.

· • · • ● · • · •

Participant Journal

The women will use the Participant Journal for notes and to record what they hear from God, answer questions, and dig deeper into Scripture. Below is a brief description of the Participant Journal's content to review with the class.

Character Builder

You will present one character quality each session to encourage the development of godly character. This section includes probing questions and an action step to help the women put the quality into practice. We recommend incorporating these character qualities into your opening remarks.

Homework

These activities and questions are designed to help each woman process what God is saying to her and to help her understand the material presented in class. These assignments are completed on the participants' own time and shared at the following session.

Personal Reflection

These thought-provoking questions prepare the participants' hearts for the content of the upcoming session. They are designed to open a dialogue between the women and God.

The *Promise Principle*

The Promise Principle is a Bible study technique developed by Phillip Hunter to teach believers how to study Scripture more thoroughly. This tool will help the women understand who God is and how His promises are the keys to finding His provision and presence in their lives.

・●・・●・・●・

Leader Coaching Note

The Promise Principle *technique may be new to the women in your class. The following pages include instructions for using the technique as well as three examples. You may incorporate these into your teaching in any way you see fit. We recommend sharing the technique instructions during Session 1 and then referring to the examples throughout the WILD course.*

・●・・●・・●・

Page 16 in the Participant Journal

(The following excerpts are taken from *The Promise Principle Journal*.)

Study Technique

The *Promise Principle* is based on 2 Peter 1:3–11. God has given us His promises to participate in His nature rather than live in our own nature. Our nature is to be ruled by our circumstances.

> In view of all this, make every effort to respond to God's promises (2 Peter 1:5 NLT).

How can I identify God's promises?

His promises are either a truth or a commandment.

How do I respond to God's promises?

1. Ask by faith (Matthew 21:22; James 4:2b)
2. Receive with thanks (1 Timothy 4:4; Ephesians 5:20)

Every truth and commandment is a promise from God. As you read, underline every promise from God and ask yourself if this is a promise you should ask God for in faith or receive with a thankful heart. Then pray it!

> Pray about everything (Philippians 4:6 NLT).

Example #1 from Ephesians

> God decided in advance to adopt us into his own family by bringing us to himself through Jesus Christ. This is what he wanted to do, and it gave him great pleasure (Ephesians 1:5 NLT).

Is this a promise you should ask for in faith or receive with thanks?
Receive with thanks!
Ask the Holy Spirit how you need to respond to this promise based on the circumstances in your life. Then pray it.

> *Lord, there are times when I feel unloved and struggle with loneliness, but I thank You that You picked me and made me a part of Your family. I am loved by You. I belong! Thank You that You desire me, Amen.*

Example #2 from Ephesians

> Asking God, the glorious Father of our Lord Jesus Christ, to give you spiritual wisdom and insight so that you might grow in your knowledge of God. I pray that your hearts will be flooded with light so that you can understand the confident hope he has given to those he called—his holy people who are his rich and glorious inheritance (Ephesians 1:17–18 NLT).

Is this a promise you should ask for in faith or receive with thanks?
Ask for by faith!
Ask the Holy Spirit how you need to respond to this promise based on the circumstances in your life. Then pray it.

> *Lord, I want to know You and all that You have for me. I ask You to give me spiritual wisdom and insight. My desire is to grow in my knowledge of You. I need to know You because I feel despair, I am anxious, and I am filled with fear. Would You fill my heart with light and overcome the darkness? Help me to understand the hope that I have in You. I want You to be my confidence, Amen.*

Recap
1. Underline the promises as you read.
2. Identify the promise as a truth or a commandment.
3. Ask the Holy Spirit what circumstance in your life is touched by this promise.
4. Do you need to ask, do you need to receive it, or both?
5. Pray it!
6. Journal what the Holy Spirit is saying to you.

SESSION 1

Leader Notes

GRACE AND PEACE BE MULTIPLIED TO YOU *in the knowledge of God and of* **JESUS OUR LORD**; SEEING THAT HIS DIVINE POWER *has granted to us everything* PERTAINING TO LIFE AND GODLINESS, THROUGH THE **TRUE KNOWLEDGE** OF HIM *Who called us by His own glory and excellence.* FOR BY THESE HE HAS GRANTED TO US *His precious and magnificent promises,* SO THAT BY THEM YOU MAY BECOME **PARTAKERS** *of the* DIVINE NATURE

· 2 PETER 1:2-4 (NASB) ·

Leader Instructions

Read 2 Peter 1:2–4 out loud to the women.

Grace and peace be multiplied to you in the knowledge of God and of Jesus our Lord; seeing that His divine power has granted to us everything pertaining to life and godliness, through the true knowledge of Him who called us by His own glory and excellence. For by these He has granted to us His precious and magnificent promises, so that by them you may become partakers of *the* divine nature (2 Peter 1:2–4 NASB).

SESSION 1

Homework: Practice Personal Reflection

Page 25 in the Participant Journal

・・・•・・・

Leader Coaching Note

This is the first instance of Personal Reflection in the WILD curriculum. Personal Reflection is a great tool to help the women grow in an ongoing pattern of dialogue with God about matters of their hearts.

Beginning in Session 2, participants will receive additional homework assignments to be completed on their own time and shared at the following session. These assignments will consist of activities and questions designed to help the women process what God is saying to them and assist in their understanding of the material being presented in class.

・・・•・・・

Leader Instructions

Explain the purpose of Personal Reflection and read the Participant Instructions (see below) out loud. Answer questions as time permits.

Participant Instructions

These thought-provoking questions are designed to be used during your personal quiet times to prepare your heart for the upcoming session.

1. **What are you asking God for in this class? Make a list of your responses.**
2. **In what area(s) of your life would you like to see growth in leadership?**
3. **Where would you like to serve?**

The *Promise Principle*

Page 28 in the Participant Journal

· • · • ● · • · • ·

Leader Coaching Note
You may incorporate this exercise into your teaching time or encourage the women to use it in their personal quiet times.

· • · • ● · • · • ·

Leader Instructions

If time permits, read the Participant Instructions (see below) out loud and answer any questions.

Participant Instructions
Read Ephesians 1

1. Underline the promises as you read.
2. Identify the promise as a truth or a commandment.
3. Ask the Holy Spirit what circumstance in your life is touched by this promise.
4. Do you need to ask, do you need to receive it, or both?
5. Pray it!
6. Journal what the Holy Spirit is saying to you.

Now ask yourself:
- What characteristics of God did I discover?
- What does this say about the character of God?

session 2

GOD CREATED MAN IN HIS OWN IMAGE, *in the image of God* HE CREATED HIM; MALE AND FEMALE *He created them.*

GENESIS 1:27 (NASB)

Session 2

· • · · • · · •

Leader Coaching Note

Impart the DNA for leadership and encourage the women to embrace an identity based on how God sees them. Inspire and challenge them to hear Him, believe what He says, and obey His voice. Help them understand how their security and confidence are found in knowing God.

· • · · • · · •

Agenda

	8–10 Participants *(75 Minutes)*	11–20 Participants *(120 Minutes)*
Welcome/Greet/Prayer	5 minutes	5 minutes
Teaching 1: Identity in Christ	20 minutes	35 minutes
Activation: Who Do You Say I Am?	20 minutes	35 minutes
Teaching 2: Core Values & Qualities of Effective Leaders	20 minutes	35 minutes
Homework Explanation: Project Development	5 minutes	5 minutes
Closing Prayer	5 minutes	5 minutes

Character Builder
INTEGRITY

Page 33 in the Participant Journal

Definition

- The ability to embrace situations, challenges, successes, pain, or areas needing growth and meet the demand of the moment
- Engaging the ability to move forward without going around, dismissing, or burying the obstacle at hand

Reading

Esther 4:4–16

Biblical Application

Esther dug deep within herself to find the courage, strength, and faith to face the king. She rose to the challenge and found her confidence in God to do what the moment required of her. Esther chose to do the right thing despite the potential consequences.

Personal Application

- Think of a time when you failed to keep a commitment. Why did you decide not to follow through?
- In the future, what would you do to avoid the same mistakes?
- Are there situations or relationships in your life today that require resolution? Maybe you have a difficult conversation you have been avoiding?
- How will you commit to addressing it?
- Focus on the worst first! You will be energized, strengthened, and find fresh motivation when you eliminate the weight and stress you are carrying around by procrastinating.

SESSION 2

Teaching 1: Identity in Christ

Page 36 in the Participant Journal

Leader Coaching Note

Your goal is to help the women understand the benefits of salvation, the importance of knowing who they are in Christ, and the authority they have as believers. Even more, help them understand the way God sees them. These truths will form the foundation upon which every teaching, activation, and homework assignment will be built.

Who Am I in Christ?

2 Corinthians 5:16–21; Ephesians 2:10

I Am Accepted

John 1:12	I am God's child.
Romans 5:1	I have been justified.
Colossians 1:14	I have been redeemed and forgiven.

I Am Secure

Romans 8:1–2	I am free forever from condemnation.
Philippians 3:20	I am a citizen of heaven.
1 John 5:18	I am born of God; the evil one cannot touch me.

I Am Significant

Matthew 5:13–14	I am the salt of the earth and the light of the world.
1 Corinthians 3:16	I am God's temple.
Ephesians 2:10	I am God's workmanship.

SESSION 2

Recommended Reading

Page 39 in the Participant Journal

Today Matters: 12 Daily Practices to Guarantee Tomorrow's Success by John Maxwell

From Dream to Destiny: The Ten Tests You Must Go Through to Fulfill God's Purpose for Your Life by Robert Morris

WILD LEADER GUIDE

Activation: Who Do You Say I Am?

Page 40 in the Participant Journal

• • • • • •

Leader Coaching Note

The participants have now reached a critical moment in their WILD experience. You are helping these women grasp their identities in Christ by talking to God for themselves. Throughout this session, they will use a question to begin a dialogue with God. The women will learn to speak to God and listen to Him at various moments. They will also share their own spiritual thoughts and ideas. This exercise builds confidence and transparency in each participant. Your teaching has spoken truth to them about their identity according to God's Word. Now they will receive personal revelations.

Some of the women may be new to the concept of asking God a question, hearing a thought or response, writing it down, and then expressing it to others immediately. They may have concerns they will not hear God. In addition, they may also feel especially vulnerable because they are being asked to reveal something personal and private about themselves which they haven't had much time to think about. This is often a breakthrough moment in which the women can be affirmed immediately for their ability to hear God and communicate what they are hearing.

• • • • • •

Leader Instructions

Read the Participant Instructions (see below) out loud.

Participant Instructions

Take five minutes of quiet time to ask God the questions below. Write down what you hear God saying to you and any Scriptures that He may give you.

1. **Who do You say I am?**
2. **What plans do You have for me?**

Leader Instructions

After the five minutes of quiet time, say to the participants,

"Begin today believing that this is who you really are. What God says about you is the truth, and He will be faithful to you. Your decision to believe and accept what He says about you opens the way for Him to prosper you and for you to experience all that He has planned for you."

Next, ask the women to take turns coming to the front of the class and sharing what they just heard from God. Remember to create a supportive, safe environment. Ask them to keep their time brief and focus on the revelation they just received, perhaps one or two minutes each. Give positive feedback and encouragement.

"And Jesus called them to him and said to them, "You know that those who are considered rulers of the Gentiles lord it over them, and their great ones exercise authority over them. But it shall not be so among you. But whoever would be great among you must be your servant, and whoever would be first among you must be slave of all. For even the Son of Man came not to be served but to serve, and to give his life as a ransom for many."

Mark 10:42-45 (ESV)

SESSION 2

Teaching 2: Core Values & Qualities of Effective Leaders

Page 42 in the Participant Journal

Leader Coaching Note

As a leader, you set the tone as a believer, wife, mother, friend, volunteer, employee, and any other capacity in which God has called you to serve. Your character will be tested, and you must know you are ready before that time comes. Included here is a list of the 12 core values of Gateway Church. We use them as a guideline for effective leadership.

Introduction

Why are core values important?
What values are you going to need to have when adversity comes?
What do you think you can do now to start building those value "muscles"?

Core Values

Take the time to study godly character so you can discover what God has to say to you about each one of these values. In this class, we will focus on humility, integrity, service, excellence, unity, and submission. We do not intend for the focus on core values to bring condemnation; rather, we present them to encourage growth. As a leader, your goal should be to develop Christ-like character in yourself and others.

Unity	Psalm 133; Hebrews 12:14
Excellence	Matthew 5:16
Humility	James 4:6
Service	Ezekiel 44; Matthew 20:28; John 13
Faith	Hebrews 11:6
Equity	Jeremiah 22:13–16; James 2:1–4
Compassion	Philippians 4:5; Matthew 20:34
Submission	Romans 13:1; Ephesians 5:21
Integrity	Philippians 2:15
Generosity	2 Corinthians 8:6
Kingdom Mindset	1 Corinthians 12:14–27
Truth and Spirit Centered	John 1, 14, 16

If your gift is to encourage others, be encouraging. If it is giving, give generously. If God has given you leadership ability, take the responsibility seriously. And if you have a gift for showing kindness to others, do it gladly.

— Romans 12:8 (NLT)

Qualities of Effective Leaders

Leader Coaching Note

A team can only follow where the leader leads. There is no greater example of leadership than Jesus Himself. It is our responsibility to follow Him and lead others to Him. The purpose of WILD is not to gain credibility, grow our own following, or create a name for ourselves. Jesus knew who He was and His purpose. Regardless of the situation, His character stayed the same. Jesus kept a close relationship with His followers and wasn't afraid of what others thought. He led selflessly, tirelessly, and wholeheartedly. Jesus also knew when to draw away to spend time alone with His Father. While we cannot hope to be perfect, isn't it wonderful to have a leader who was? People tend to rise to the standard set by their leaders. As a leader, you are not only accountable to someone else, but you can also help those who follow your lead accept accountability.

Leader Instructions

Tell the women most of the qualities below are addressed in more detail through the Character Builder exercises found in the Participant Journal.

1. Effective Leaders Build Unity

Unity: A condition of harmony and accord

"A new commandment I give to you, that you love one another; as I have loved you, that you also love one another. By this all will know that you are My disciples, if you have love for one another" (John 13:34–35).

"Therefore if you bring your gift to the altar, and there remember that your brother has something against you, leave your gift there before the altar, and go your way. First be reconciled to your brother, and then come and offer your gift" (Matthew 5:23–24).

> Behold, how good and how pleasant *it is*
> For brethren to dwell together in unity!
> ... For there the Lord commanded the blessing—
> Life forevermore (Psalm 133:1,3).

> Pursue peace with all people (Hebrews 12:14).

Offenses and differences can easily divide us. The devil wants us to act spitefully, feel misunderstood, and create division. If he can distract us, he will lead us into an endless cycle of hurt and broken relationships. Leaders need to create a culture of unity. God designed us to live in relationship with one another—we are better together. By building each other up, we make ourselves stronger as a whole and receive God's favor.

2. Effective Leaders Strive for Excellence

Excellence: The quality of being outstanding or extremely good

Excellence does not set us up for never being "good enough." Rather, it encourages us to bring our best efforts, to be "all in." Excellence allows us to give our best and be our best; however, we should understand that if we mess up and forget something, grace is available. Recognize that God gave you gifts to enable you to excel in some things but also be aware that you are not better than others in God's eyes.

3. Effective Leaders Are Humble

Humble: Not full of pride or having an excessive appreciation of oneself

Humble leaders are not haughty or arrogant. We should not deflect praise in false humility but give credit where credit is due, which allows God to receive the glory for the way He made us. God created you in an amazing way!

4. Effective Leaders Have Integrity

Integrity: Firm adherence to a code of (especially) moral values; the quality or state of being complete

The confidence, strength, and character defined as *integrity* come through the security found in knowing God and having an intimate relationship with Him. If you know your boundaries before you face a challenge, you will be able to make hard yet godly decisions amid difficult circumstances. Jesus was the same in every situation. He knew how to respond regardless of what was happening around Him. He could do this because He was a man of integrity. Jesus knew His standards and acted according to them in every situation.

5. Effective Leaders Serve

Serve: To act in a way that will help or benefit others without expectation of reward

Servant leadership is a biblical concept seen in the life of Jesus. Rather than being overly concerned with our title or position, we should be focused on demonstrating a life dedicated to the good of others. In Acts 6, the early church selected seven men to oversee the daily serving of food to those in need. These men were "of *good* reputation, full of the Holy spirit and wisdom" (Acts 6:3).

> "If anyone desires to be first, he shall be last of all and servant of all" (Mark 9:35).

> But Jesus called them to Himself and said to them, "You know that those who are considered rulers over the Gentiles lord it over them, and their great ones exercise authority over them. Yet it shall not be so among you; but whoever desires to become great among you shall be your servant. And whoever of you desires to be first shall be slave of all. For even the Son of Man did not come to be served, but to serve, and to give His life a ransom for many" (Mark 10:42–45).

> Also see Philippians 2:5–7 and Colossians 3:23–24.

But I do not consider my life of any account as dear to myself, so that I may finish my course and the ministry which I received from the Lord Jesus, to testify solemnly of the gospel of the grace of God.

Acts 20:24 (NASB)

Homework: Project Development

Page 58 in the Participant Journal

· • · ● · • ·

Leader Coaching Note

The participants will develop a five-minute project on the topic of their choice to present during Session 6. By introducing the assignment in Session 2, you allow the women to have four full sessions to pray about their projects and complete them. The project may cause some initial anxiety for the participants—it may seem unusual to be asked to present a project without a clear statement of expectations. Encourage the women by telling them anything they have on their hearts is acceptable. Their only limitation is time.

· • · ● · • ·

Leader Instructions

Introduce the project assignment by reading the Participant Instructions (see below) out loud. The women will likely have questions, so answer as many as time permits. Offer to stay after class to answer any additional questions.

Participant Instructions

In Session 6, you will present a five-minute project. It should be born out of your own heart and passion. You can determine the scope, delivery, and content.

Women in previous WILD classes have presented projects that included sermons, book outlines, magazine articles, devotionals, mission trip plans, governmental recommendations for establishing ministries, music, painting, and art. You have no limits on the scope of your project. You can choose something practical. You can display your gifts to express what God is teaching you. Or you can select something fun. You have the freedom to use any type of prop, visual aid, music, or handout that you find helpful.

Your project may be a small portion of a bigger vision. For example, you could develop an outline for a book instead of writing the entire book. You could present a selection of an extended article for a magazine. You could preach one point out of a three-point sermon. The goal is not so much the completion but the birth of something new in you.

On project day, you will present your thoughts within a five-minute time limit. Please prepare carefully so that you have an opportunity to communicate your ideas fully and passionately within the restricted time limit. If possible, please give a digital copy of your notes or project to your leader to keep.

Personal Reflection

Page 60 in the Participant Journal

1. **How does it feel to know that you are special to God and that He has a purpose for your life?**
2. **Make a list of reasons why you might feel inadequate.**
3. **Make a list of God's promises over you and your future.**
4. **How do these promises give you courage and strength?**

The *Promise Principle*

Page 64 in the Participant Journal

Read Ephesians 2
1. Underline the promises as you read.
2. Identify the promise as a truth or a commandment.
3. Ask the Holy Spirit what circumstance in your life is touched by this promise.
4. Do you need to ask, do you need to receive it, or both?
5. Pray it!
6. Journal what the Holy Spirit is saying to you.

Now ask yourself:
- What characteristics of God did I discover?
- What does this say about the character of God?

session 3

NEVER BE LACKING IN ZEAL, *but keep your spiritual fervor,* **SERVING THE LORD.**

ROMANS 12:11 (NIV)

Session 3

· • · • ● · • · • ·

Leader Coaching Note

Inspire the women to pursue true heart transformations in which they will learn to serve others and silence the voice of comparison. As a woman discovers her real identity, she can embrace the truth that her unique gifts are tools to help her fulfill the unique plan God has for her life.

· • · • ● · • · • ·

Agenda

	8–10 Participants (75 Minutes)	11–20 Participants (120 Minutes)
Welcome/Greet/Prayer	5 minutes	5 minutes
Teaching 1: Finding Your Passion	20 minutes	30 minutes
Activation: Share the Gifts You See in Others	20 minutes	40 minutes
Teaching 2: Comparison	20 minutes	30 minutes
Activation: Breaking Comparison & Affirming Identity in Christ	5 minutes	10 minutes
Homework Explanation & Closing Prayer	5 minutes	5 minutes

Character Builder
SERVICE

Page 69 in the Participant Journal

Definition

- Assisting others with an attitude or desire to benefit them and to see them succeed

    Let each of you look not only to his own interests, but also to the interests of others (Philippians 2:4 ESV).

Reading

The book of Ruth

Biblical Application

Ruth set aside her family and her own needs and left everything to serve Naomi. She followed Naomi's advice regardless of the cost. Ruth served and worked long hours in the field to gather food for herself and Naomi.

Personal Application

List any areas of your life where you have been unwilling to help others.

- Why have you resisted giving to others?
- Think of a time when you resisted being sensitive to others who wanted or needed your help.
- How did that experience make you feel?
- How is God asking you to respond?
- Think and pray about the issues that are keeping you from having a servant's heart and choose one person to serve this week.

SESSION 3

Teaching 1: Finding Your Passion

Page 72 in the Participant Journal

• • • ● • • •

Leader Coaching Note

Once a woman understands her identity in Christ, it's time for her to explore what makes her unique. This teaching begins with a discussion of the power and importance of passion for the individual believer. You will look beneath obvious or common passions (like family, food, or fun) and dig down deep to find the roots of the participants' callings. Encourage the women to examine and explore their hearts so they can hear from God and clearly understand their personal passions. Once they agree with God about what makes them tick, they can begin to see themselves as leaders. These revelations will jumpstart their journeys of self-discovery and give them endless supplies of energy and purpose. You will also begin to see their leadership interests and potentials emerge.

• • • ● • • •

1. What is Passion?

Passion comes from powerful emotions (such as love, joy, hate, and anger) and boundless enthusiasm. It is your zeal in life and the fuel that enables you to change the world. *True passion will pull destiny from you.*

2. Why is Passion Important?

Discovering your core passions and understanding their importance will be a lifelong self-discovery process. When you unearth the gold mine of passion, you will find an endless supply of energy and purpose.

3. How Do I Find My Passion?

Passion is born out of experience. First, you have an experience; then you feel the passion. You will discover your passion as you put yourself in a position to have a burning bush experience. Turn aside, consider things that are really important to you, and ask God about His purpose for your life. Do something new. Follow your curiosity and explore your world. Look around until you discover the things you feel strongly about.

4. Where Do I Start?

Begin with what you know. Make choices based on what you already like. Likes can turn into passions, but they start as interests. Also, make some choices based on the things which really bother you or which you dislike. Do you find yourself thinking, "This bothers me so much—I want to help change it!"? As you find something you want to change or something you want to be a part of, you are getting closer to your passion.

5. What Do I Do Once I Find My Passion?

- Set goals to prepare for what's to come. Goals are powerful motivators and will take you places you never imagined. They will open the journey and plunge you into a current that will carry you to your destiny.
- Don't try to predict the path your journey will take. You can only begin and allow your passions to evolve.
- Start now! Take small steps toward your destiny. Whatever God puts in your hands today needs to be developed for tomorrow.
- Writers: blog or journal.
- Speakers: develop a message. Find opportunities to practice speaking, even if it is to yourself in the mirror. Look for openings to pour God's message into others.

SESSION 3

Activation: Share the Gifts You See in Others

Page 77 in the Participant Journal

· • · • ● • · • ·

Leader Coaching Note

This activation is designed to open the women's eyes to the gifts in others while also helping them overcome the temptation of comparison. We often struggle to celebrate the gifts in others because we are too busy thinking about whether we are better or worse than they are. We fail to recognize or appreciate our own gifts. This exercise will open the women's hearts to each other and create an environment that celebrates their uniqueness and prepares them for the upcoming teaching on comparison.

· • · • ● • · • ·

Leader Instructions

Read the Participant Instructions (see below) out loud.

Participant Instructions

Gather in groups of three or four. Take a few minutes to write down the gifts and spiritual fruits you see in the lives of the women in your group.

Now take three minutes each to share with your group what you have written about each other.

Therefore, since we are surrounded by such a huge crowd of witnesses to the life of faith, let us strip off every weight that slows us down, especially the sin that so easily trips us up. And let us run with endurance the race God has set before us. We do this by keeping our eyes on Jesus, the champion who initiates and perfects our faith. Because of the joy awaiting him, he endured the cross, disregarding its shame. Now he is seated in the place of honor beside God's throne.

Hebrews 12:1-2 (NLT)

SESSION 3

Teaching 2: Comparison

Page 80 in the Participant Journal

· • · ● · • ·

Leader Coaching Note

You are leading the women on a journey of self-discovery by encouraging them to hear God and recognize their unique passions. You have given them an opportunity to share and communicate these exciting discoveries. The temptation to compare is a natural byproduct of this process. Comparison will kill a woman's passion and convince her that other people's gifts are more valuable, beautiful, or exciting. In this teaching, you will expose this thinking pattern. Encourage the women to break free from the tendency to compare. Inspire them to build a culture that celebrates the unique gifts and talents of each person.

· • · ● · • ·

1. Run *Your* Race

The race you run is specific to you, custom designed by God for you (Ephesians 2:10). You also have specific gifts and talents that are uniquely yours (1 Peter 4:10; 1 Corinthians 12:14–18).

Never quit (Galatians 6:9). *All* of us have bumps in the road of life, but we must keep going (John 16:33). Looking back will make you want to quit (Isaiah 43:18), so surround yourself with those who will cheer you on (1 Thessalonians 5:11).

2. Comparison Produces the Wrong Fruit in Our Lives

One of the main hindrances to running your race is *comparison*. Comparison happens when you *examine the character qualities of something or someone in order to discover resemblances or differences.*

Here are the ways we compare:

- With others (physically, financially, spiritually)
- With our own ideas (where we *think* we should be in life)

Comparison is dangerous (John 10:10). It is a scheme of the enemy. In the beginning, he used comparison to trick Eve.

Here is what comparison will do:

- **Steal** your peace, joy, and happiness
- **Kill** your dreams and desires
- **Destroy** your security, your confidence, and who God created you to be
- **Create** insecurity, resentment, and bitterness

3. K.I.C.K. Comparison to the Curb

*K*now who and Whose you are!

- **The Word**: Psalm 139:16–17; Ephesians 1:4–6
- **Prayer**: Jeremiah 29:12
- **Worship**: Psalm 97:5

*I*dentify which voices you are listening to.

- There are three different voices.
    - **Satan's voice**: Revelation 12:9; Matthew 4:5–7
    - **Your own voice**: Jeremiah 17:9
    - **God's voice**: John 1:14
- Identify the voice by arresting the thought and asking yourself if it agrees with God's Word.

*C*ounter the enemy's voice with God's Word.

- 2 Corinthians 10:5
- Romans 12:2

*K*eep the cycle going!

- Continue to kick comparison to the curb by repeating the K.I.C.K. steps.

Activation: Breaking Comparison & Affirming Identity in Christ

Page 85 in the Participant Journal

Leader Instructions

This is a special time to minister to the women in your class. Lead them in a prayer of repentance that breaks their agreement with comparison. Then lead them to receive and affirm their individual identities in Christ. You can invite the women to pray for one another in groups or set aside several minutes of quiet time for personal repentance and prayer. Do not rush this exercise; take your time and make it memorable and effective. You are doing a significant spiritual work while the women are tender toward themselves and each other.

SESSION 3

Homework: What Is My Passion?

Page 87 in the Participant Journal

• • • ● • • •

Leader Coaching Note

This is a prophetic exercise designed to help the participants confirm their ability to hear God personally. It may create some distress since many of the women have likely never been asked to examine their hearts, gifts, and values to determine what is most important to them. Prepare to encourage the participants and keep pressing them to turn to God for their answers. This assignment will open the shells of their hearts as it asks them to be transparent and self-aware.

• • • ● • • •

Leader Instructions

Explain the purpose of the passion assignment and read the Participant Instructions (see below) out loud. Answer questions as time permits.

Participant Instructions

Prepare a two-minute presentation on your passion to present to the class during the next session. Use the following questions as you brainstorm possible passions.

1. **What are my goals?**
2. **What do I love to do?**
3. **If I could do one thing for the rest of my life, what would it be?**
4. **What would I do even if I didn't get paid to do it?**

Personal Reflection

Page 91 in the Participant Journal

1. **Are you presenting your thoughts clearly to family, friends, and coworkers?**
2. **Is there anything distracting in the manner you are using to present?**
3. **Do you keep eye contact? Is it enough or too much?**

The *Promise Principle*

Page 94 in the Participant Journal

Read Ephesians 3

1. Underline the promises as you read.
2. Identify the promise as a truth or a commandment.
3. Ask the Holy Spirit what circumstance in your life is touched by this promise.
4. Do you need to ask, do you need to receive it, or both?
5. Pray it!
6. Journal what the Holy Spirit is saying to you.

Now ask yourself:

- What characteristics of God did I discover?
- What does this say about the character of God?

Session 4

DEAR BROTHERS AND SISTERS, NOT MANY OF YOU SHOULD BECOME TEACHERS IN THE CHURCH, *for we who teach* WILL BE JUDGED MORE STRICTLY.

— JAMES 3:1 (NLT)

Session 4

· · • • • · ·

Leader Coaching Note

God calls each of us to give testimony to the things He has done. Encourage the women to find their voices and remove any distractions. They will learn to conquer nervousness, fear, and negative body language.

· · • • • · ·

Agenda

	8–10 Participants *(75 Minutes)*	11–20 Participants *(120 Minutes)*
Welcome/Greet/Prayer	5 minutes	5 minutes
Activation: Passion Presentations	25 minutes	60 minutes
Teaching 1: Speaking Tips	15 minutes	20 minutes
Activation: Practice Speaking Skills	5 minutes	5 minutes
Teaching 2: Writing Tips	20 minutes	25 minutes
Homework Explanation & Closing Prayer	5 minutes	5 minutes

Character Builder
EXCELLENCE

Page 99 in the Participant Journal

Definition

- The quality of being outstanding or extremely good
- Not perfection, but rather doing your very best and giving your best in all you put your hands and heart to

And whatever you do in word or deed, do all in the name of the Lord Jesus, giving thanks to God the Father through Him (Colossians 3:17).

Reading

Colossians 3:17, 22; Philippians 2:1–8; Galatians 1:10; Ephesians 6:5–6

Biblical Application

The apostle Paul is an example of living with a standard of excellence. He called himself a "bondservant" in reverence for the Lord and lived his life to obtain "an imperishable *crown*" (1 Corinthians 9:24–25).

Personal Application

Think of any areas where you have not given your best.

- How did it affect the outcome?
- What steps do you need to take to give your best to all you do?
- What is the Holy Spirit saying to you?

Activation: Passion Presentations

Page 102 in the Participant Journal

• • • ● • • •

Leader Coaching Note

You are about to learn some amazing things about the women in your class. Hopefully they are becoming ever more comfortable with sharing publicly what God is saying to them privately. You may witness tears, laughter, hugs, and expressions of agreement. It is very vulnerable for the participants to share something God has spoken to them about themselves. Remember to create an atmosphere of safety and give immediate affirmation.

• • • ● • • •

Leader Instructions

- Begin the exercise with a brief review of the homework assignment.
- Create a sense of excitement and anticipation.
- Invite each woman to come forward and share her passion in two minutes or less.
- Take good notes and ask the Holy Spirit to help you see each woman with His eyes.
- Remember to affirm and offer personal encouragement when each woman finishes sharing.

Teaching 1: Speaking Tips

Page 104 in the Participant Journal

· • · • ● • · • ·

Leader Coaching Note

Many people are terrified of public speaking. These are practical tips to give the women confidence and help them break through this fear so they will be free to express themselves. It is important for leaders to communicate well. Leaders may have great content and wisdom, but if their delivery style is distracting, it will compromise their message and credibility. Whether the participants will be sharing their stories across a table, or their opinions in a board room, or teaching from a platform, they need to communicate clearly and effectively. This teaching focuses on simple yet practical tips the women can immediately use to practice their speaking skills in class.

· • · • ● • · • ·

General Tips

- Be prepared. Organize your speech: topic, purpose, central ideas, and main points.
- Gain attention at the beginning.
- Know your audience. The speech is about them. Adapt your material and the words you use to the audience.
- Research the environment where you will speak and prepare accordingly.
- Practice. Nervousness is normal. Practice and preparation will help you overcome anxiety.
- Be yourself. Choose your style and become exceptional at it.
- Be passionate but also be genuine. You are there to deliver a message and make a point, not to put on a show.
- Finish strong.

Verbal Expression—How We Speak Matters

- Don't start speaking until you have taken your place in front of the group. Take a deep breath and then begin.
- Vary the volume of your voice for effect.
- Speak more slowly than you usually would. People tend to increase the speed of their words when they are in front of a group.
- Vary the pace of your speech. Be energetic but don't yell.
- Slow down or pause for a dramatic effect. The audience will anticipate the importance of what you are about to say or the importance of what you just said.
- Be clear and concise. Use concrete terms and familiar words.
- Speak smoothly. Avoid the use of speech breaks like "*uhh*" or "*umm*."
- Use vivid language, including active verbs and superlative adjectives and adverbs. Instead of *good, great,* and *fine,* use words such as *wonderful, excellent,* and *fantastic.*
- Enunciate. Be clear and crisp with your words. Regional dialects can be distracting. Ask a friend to write down every word you say that sounds funny.
- Stories, examples, and interesting facts are useful tools, especially as an introduction. Avoid the use of jokes or humor unless you are quite comfortable with them and you are certain they are appropriate for the audience.
- Change your inflection by accentuating words or phrases.

Body Language

- Maintain good posture. You should be equally balanced on both feet.
- Avoid using many large, exaggerated gestures. These should be used sparingly and briefly. Use gestures and facial expressions that support your story. Gestures are particularly useful for acting out verbs. You can act them out with your hands, face, and body. Your face reflects your

emotions. Telling a painful story with a broad smile will not convey your message well. Tailor your gestures to the type and size of the audience.
- Your body posture and gestures should match your words.

Eye Contact

- Make eye contact. Remember, your countenance is dominated by your eyes.
- Make eye contact with one person at a time. Finish your sentence or point before you move your eyes.
- Your eyes "grab" the audience. Don't move your head rapidly—this is not a tennis match.
- Purposeful eye contact makes people feel like they are part of what you are sharing.

Staging

- You want your audience to see Jesus rather than you.
- Consider the venue and set-up in advance. Find out how you can connect by being close to the audience.
- Small rooms require less movement, but eye contact becomes even more important.
- If you stand behind a podium, you will need to compensate by moving your eyes, face, and arms slowly and intentionally.

Recommended Reading

Page 116 in the Participant Journal

Speak with Confidence: Powerful Presentations That Inform, Inspire and Persuade by Dianna Booher

Communicating for a Change: Seven Keys to Irresistible Communication by Andy Stanley and Lane Jones

Activation: Practice Speaking Skills

Page 117 in the Participant Journal

Leader Instructions

Read the Participant Instructions (see below) out loud. You may select a single volunteer to perform the exercise or have the group recite it together.

Participant Instructions

Read the following phrases out loud, being careful to place emphasis on each bold word.

> **THE** Lord is my Shepherd.
> The **LORD** is my Shepherd.
> The Lord **IS** my Shepherd.
> The Lord is **MY** Shepherd.
> The Lord is my **SHEPHERD.**

Optional Leader Instructions

If time permits, allow each participant to give a one-minute speech on the topic of her choice. Give constructive feedback regarding posture, facial expressions, enunciation, etc.

And the Lord answered me: "Write the vision; make it plain on tablets, so he may run who reads it."

— Habakkuk 2:2 (ESV)

Teaching 2: Writing Tips

Page 119 in the Participant Journal

• • • ● • • •

Leader Coaching Note

Leaders should be able to speak effectively, but it is just as important to communicate well through writing. The written word is a powerful medium that reaches people you may never meet face-to-face. It is also an indispensable mentoring tool. Thanks to current technology, writing has become accessible to people everywhere. The women in your class have testimonies and messages only they can share. Writing gives them a platform to communicate their unique journeys with passion and excellence. This teaching includes some simple tips to help the women get started, followed by a homework assignment to activate their writing skills.

• • • ● • • •

Leader Instructions

Begin by asking, "What fears or concerns do you have about the practice of writing?" Get a few of the women to respond. Then share these tips to help the participants overcome concerns and hindrances.

Write About What You Know

- Be yourself. Nobody can argue with your personal experiences.
- Sharing your own experiences will show honesty and sincerity.
- Write about what inspires you or changed you and how others can apply it to their lives.

Organize Your Work

- Start with an outline.
- Decide on the topic, purpose, central ideas, and main points of the piece. You can develop the introduction and closing later.
- State your purpose. For example, are you trying to impart information primarily for learning, or are you trying to inspire and motivate your listeners to action?
- Start by writing creatively in a way that captures the heart and purpose of your piece.
- Leave editing for later.

Brainstorm (The Wagon Wheel)

· • • ● • • ·

Leader Coaching Note

There is a Wagon Wheel graphic on page 85 in this Leader Guide. It is page 134 in the Participant Journal. If time permits, pause at this point in the teaching and allow the women to try out their Wagon Wheel after reading the following Participant Instructions.

· • • ● • • ·

Participant Instructions

There is a Wagon Wheel graphic on page 134. The main idea or thought is the center hub of the wheel, and as points become apparent, they will become the various spokes. Use the illustration as a reference and draw your own wagon wheel on scratch paper. It doesn't have to be perfect!

- All good writing begins with the development of a central thought, which the writer then supports with facts, illustrations, examples, or ideas.
- The benefit of using brainstorming as a writing tool is that you can keep, cut, or expand any idea or concept you choose.
- Brainstorming opens the creative side of an author's mind and helps her to see and develop previously unseen ideas.

Use Strong, Simple Words

Instead of	Try using
Really good	*Great*
Very beautiful	*Gorgeous*
Tired	*Exhausted*
Scared	*Terrified*
It's not that good	*It's terrible*

Consider the Reader

- Use language that suits your audience.
- Take care in using humor. Make clarity and appropriateness your priority. If English is not your audience's first language, they will not likely understand your style of humor.

Show, Don't Tell—Use the Active Voice for Verbs

Active	**Passive**
We are going to watch a movie tonight.	A movie is going to be watched by us tonight.
The forest fire destroyed the whole suburb.	The whole suburb was destroyed by the forest fire.
Susan will bake two dozen cupcakes for the bake sale.	For the bake sale, two dozen cupcakes will be baked by Susan.

If you select the grammar and spelling check in Microsoft Word, the program will reveal the percentage of passive voice verbs and readability statistics. You may need to turn on this feature if it is not enabled in the default program.

Work the Details

- Keep verb tenses consistent.
- Use parallel constructions—create patterns.
- Be accurate—check your facts.

Edit, Edit, Edit

- Be concise. Eliminate unnecessary words and phrases. Use repetition carefully.
- Use short sentences. Shorter sentences create more impact and are easier for the reader or listener to follow. Longer sentences are more complex grammatically, which can lead to errors and/or difficulty in understanding.

Choose a Title

- Use a powerful title.
- The title should reflect the purpose of the piece and relate to the interest of your readers.
- Develop your subtitles and sections (such as an overview or summary). An *Executive Summary* is always written after the work is complete.

Find an Editor and Re-edit Yourself

- Find someone who is capable of reviewing and commenting on your writing. Ask that person to compare your writing to your outline.

- Print out a hard copy.
- Read your work out loud alone or with someone else.
- Ask someone who has proofreading knowledge and experience to go over your manuscript. Proofreading is different from editing.

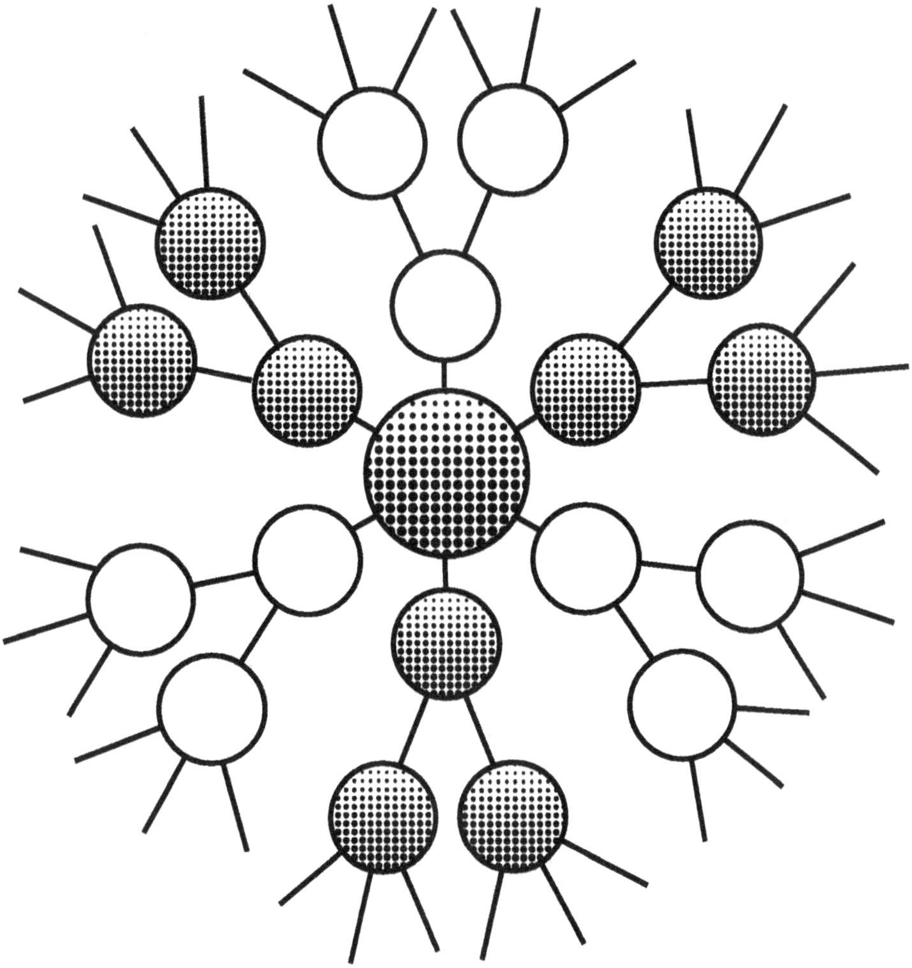

Homework: Write a Blog or Devotional

Page 135 in the Participant Journal

Leader Instructions

Introduce the writing assignment by reading the Participant Instructions (see below) out loud. Encourage the women to use the Wagon Wheel method. Answer questions as time permits.

Participant Instructions

Write a blog or devotional to share in class next session. Here are some guidelines:

- **Develop a strong title.**
- **Communicate one point or thought.**
- **Include one Scripture reference, written out (include the translation notation).**
- **Consider telling a story or using an illustration.**
- **Rather than telling the reader what to do, consider telling them what God has taught you.**

Personal Reflection

Page 139 in the Participant Journal

1. **What helps or hinders you based on your personal strengths or weaknesses in speaking or writing?**
2. **What are some things you can do to overcome hindrances?**

The *Promise Principle*

Page 141 in the Participant Journal

Read Ephesians 4

1. Underline the promises as you read.
2. Identify the promise as a truth or a commandment.
3. Ask the Holy Spirit what circumstance in your life is touched by this promise.
4. Do you need to ask, do you need to receive it, or both?
5. Pray it!
6. Journal what the Holy Spirit is saying to you.

Now ask yourself:
- What characteristics of God did I discover?
- What does this say about the character of God?

session 5

Session 5

· · · · • · · · ·

Leader Coaching Note
The most beautiful evidence of a Spirit-led leader is the fruit of the Spirit in her life. We should all encourage and love one another.

· · · · • · · · ·

Agenda

	8–10 Participants *(75 Minutes)*	**11–20 Participants** *(120 Minutes)*
Welcome/Greet/Prayer	5 minutes	5 minutes
Teaching: Spirit-Led Leaders	20 minutes	20 minutes
Activation: Share Your Blog or Devotional	30 minutes	65 minutes
Activation: Words of Encouragement	15 minutes	25 minutes
Homework Explanation & Closing Prayer	5 minutes	5 minutes

Character Builder
UNITY

Page 147 in the Participant Journal

Definition

- A condition of harmony; accord

    Bearing with one another, and forgiving one another, if anyone has a complaint against another; even as Christ forgave you, so you also must do (Colossians 3:13).

Reading

Psalm 133:1–3; Matthew 5:9; 18:15–17; Philippians 2:1–4; 2 Timothy 2:24; Ephesians 4:3

Biblical Application

Living in peace with one another is no small matter to God. In Numbers 12:1–9, God Himself shows up to deal with the divisive behavior of Aaron and Miriam. The consequences affected the whole camp of Israel, "and the people did not journey till Miriam was brought in *again*" (Numbers 12:15).

Personal Application

Simple steps to address confrontation with the purpose of unity:

- Pray.
- Soul search. Read Matthew 5:23–24; 7:3–5.
- Set your goal. What positive outcomes do you hope to achieve?
- Plan your approach. Avoid defensiveness, finger-pointing, and blame.
- Work through what you will say. Research conflict resolution and conflict management, if needed.
- Decide on the steps that will reduce negative outcomes. Remember to win the relationship rather than the argument.
- Time your confrontation carefully. Make sure there is adequate time and an appropriate atmosphere to discuss the issues. For example, don't wait until the end of the day when you and the other people involved are exhausted, which increases the potential for tempers to flare.
- Avoid using blame by focusing on how the other party's actions affect you:
  - "When you do/say _____, it makes me feel _____."
  - "Help me understand what you mean when you do/say _____."
  - "I'm sure you did not intend for your comment to _____, but that is how it felt. Is that what you meant to tell me?"
  - "I'm sorry if I misunderstood, but I heard you say _____. Is that what you meant to say?"
- Be humble, be kind, and be clear.
- How will you respond if things don't go the way you want them to or if it gets uncomfortable or confusing? If the conversation becomes too heated, it is often a good idea to take a break and commit to come back together to finish what is unresolved. You might say something like, "I really value our relationship, and resolving this means a lot to me. Let's pause and step back before we say something we regret. Let's plan to talk about this after we have both had more time to think through these issues."
- Extend grace.

Shepherd the flock of God among you, exercising oversight not under compulsion, but voluntarily, according to the will of God; and not for sordid gain, but with eagerness

1 Peter 5:2 (NASB)

Teaching: Spirit-led Leaders

Page 151 in the Participant Journal

• • • ● • • •

Leader Coaching Note

This session will end with an activation designed to stir up confidence and encourage the women in their spiritual gifts. When we receive Christ, the Holy Spirit becomes our constant companion, leading us to follow Christ with greater confidence. The ability to hear and obey are marks of a Spirit-empowered leader. This ability gives the participants confidence and courage to trust God. They will have clear insight to minister in a variety of circumstances and settings. Your responsibility is to encourage their leadership skills and create a safe environment for the women to grow.

• • • ● • • •

Introduction

God has fashioned us to need His counsel and leadership; therefore, we naturally seek to lead and be led. However, we must first submit to the leadership of the Holy Spirit. As we follow Him, the fruit of the Spirit will mark our leadership.

The Key to Practicing Spirit-led Leadership is Simple Obedience

The Bible contains many examples of common people who became great leaders because they were willing to inquire of the Lord and obey Him.

Here are three well-known examples from the Bible:
- **Moses**: In Exodus 3, Moses turned aside to see the burning bush. He had a conversation with the Lord about his calling and qualifications.
- **David**: Nine times in the books of 1 and 2 Samuel David inquired of the Lord regarding his enemies and God's plan for battle.
- **Solomon**: In 2 Chronicles 1, Solomon asked the Lord for wisdom to lead his people.

See Acts 13:2–3; 15:28; 16:6–10.

Basic Requirements of a Spirit-led Leader

1. Know Jesus (Acts 4:12–13). Salvation is a requirement before you can be led by the Holy Spirit.
2. Be able to hear His voice (John 10:27). As a follower of Christ, you can recognize His voice and follow Him.
3. Have a heart to obey (1 John 5:2). If you love God, you will keep His commandments and follow His leading.
4. Be prepared to commit (Proverbs 16:3). When you commit yourself to the Lord, He establishes your plans.

Helpful Hints

Here are some helpful hints for you to consider as you minister to others. Be aware of their needs and not just your own agenda. Focus on love and move forward carefully by being sensitive to the direction of the Holy Spirit.

1. Be sensitive to the season—yours and theirs. Don't give counsel that is out of season. Stop, look, and listen for hints about their current situation and phrase your counsel with wisdom.
2. Strengths are greater than weaknesses. Love is stronger than bondage. It is more important to love others than it is to correct their weaknesses

or expose their bondage. Encouragement and kindness provide a safe environment and foster a willingness to receive.
3. Know your leadership style, both strengths and weaknesses. Become more self-aware. Study your patterns and passions. Position yourself to lead with grace and be conscious of your own tendencies.
4. Study and emulate what you value. Find and follow the lead of someone who has a lifestyle or spiritual fruit you admire.
5. Remember, Spirit-led leadership requires sensitivity both to the Holy Spirit's voice and to the people you seek to lead. Ask these questions before you begin to minister:
    - What is my relationship with this person? Do I have the relational equity to speak into her life?
    - Is the door open or closed? Do I have permission to speak, share, or pray?
    - Is the timing right? Sometimes you will have a word of encouragement to share, but the setting or timing is wrong. Practice self-control and wait.
    - Is the response required of me natural or spiritual? People can't receive spiritual food when their natural needs are unmet. Feed the hungry. Give water to the thirsty.

Basic Principles

1. When ministering in the gifts of the Spirit, remember that God moved with compassion and intersected with our broken world to bring hope, encouragement, healing, and restoration.
2. Consider the environment. Are you in a corporate gathering, a small group, or face-to-face with an individual? Each of these settings requires a different sensitivity and delivery.
3. Can you move in the gifts in a non-spiritual environment, using non-church words? Many people are turned off by "Christianese." Jesus often spoke spiritual truths in common language.

4. Don't draw attention to yourself. Try to minister in a way that puts the focus on the work of God.
5. The fruit of the Spirit is so powerful in drawing people to the true Source of our hope. You can never overuse this simple fruit. Sometimes it is better to use fruit than gifts. After all, love never fails.
   - People respond to the fruit of the Spirit.
   - Fruit builds influence and trust.
   - The gifts of the Spirit are ministered through the fruit of the Spirit.
6. Our natural senses are mirrored in the Spirit. Learn to pay attention to all your senses so you can discern the mood and direction of the Holy Spirit.
   - The ability to see, hear, feel, smell, and taste are critical in the Spirit.
   - You must pay attention to understand the total situation. Don't lean on only one sense.
   - If you depend on just one sense, you'll miss the mark and become confused.
7. All believers are destined to mature into faithful followers of Christ. Yet sometimes we fail to thrive and instead become satisfied with an immature relationship with the Lord. If we will practice hearing and obeying, we will naturally move from our youthful experiences into full maturity.
   - As young Christians, much of our Christian walk is about conforming to God's will. Like the parent of a toddler, God will tell us "no" for our own benefit. We choose whether to obey or not.
   - As we start to mature, our desires begin to match God's heart. He no longer has to lead us primarily through restriction. Instead, we develop a relationship in which our desires and direction are matched with His.
   - As mature Christians, we may find it difficult to discern our will from God's will. This time requires greater listening and an even closer relationship.

Summary

If you practice a lifestyle of hearing and obeying God, you will have great favor and an increased capacity to hear His voice. If you combine this lifestyle with humility and a servant's heart, it will produce great influence and effectiveness in your life. If you are faithful with small steps of obedience, God will entrust you with greater and greater opportunities to obey.

IT IS NOT THIS WAY
AMONG YOU,
BUT WHOEVER WISHES
to become GREAT AMONG YOU
shall be your SERVANT.
— MATTHEW 20:26 (NASB)

Activation: Share Your Blog or Devotional

Page 163 in the Participant Journal

Leader Coaching Note
Participants often say, "I'm not a good writer." This exercise will help the women silence this lie and overcome any personal hindrances that prevent their best work. Again, you will be breaking through spiritual barriers to demonstrate how these women are capable of communicating their hearts.

Leader Instructions

Use this time for the presentation of the writing exercise the women were assigned as homework during the last session.

To have adequate time for presentations, you can ask the women to share the "story" of their writing, rather than reading the entire manuscript to the class. Also, if time is limited, allow one to two minutes per person.

SESSION 5

Activation: Words of Encouragement

Page 165 in the Participant Journal

• • • ● • • •

Leader Coaching Note
We call these activations "Popcorn Prophecy." They are simple tools to bless each woman with a shower of encouraging words and observations. The participants will both give and receive these words in a simple, flowing style of delivery. The women will build each other up and express the love of God as they practice the simple skill of giving prophetic encouragement.

• • • ● • • •

Leader Instructions

Activation 1:

- Select one woman at a time to sit in the front, facing the rest of the class.
- Tell the participants to give encouragement to each woman in one word statements as they come to mind. For example: wise, gracious, sweet, teacher, mother, encourager, leader, etc.
- Take one minute for each person to receive these "popcorn" words of encouragement.

Activation 2:

- Instruct the women to form two lines.
- The first line should give a word of encouragement or Scripture to the second line, and then the second line will do the same for the first.
- Tell each woman to move to the right until each person has encouraged four people or until time runs out.

Homework: Project Development

Page 167 in the Participant Journal

・•・●・•・

Leader Coaching Note
Encourage the women to prepare their projects carefully so they will be able to communicate their hearts within the allotted time. If possible, ask them to bring a digital copy of their presentations for you to keep.

・•・●・•・

Leader Instructions

Read the Participant Instructions (see below) out loud. Offer to stay after class to answer any questions or to help anyone who needs assistance with her project.

Participant Instructions

There is no additional homework for this session. Use the time to finalize your project that you will present during the next session. Remember to keep your presentation within a five-minute limit and come prepared with whatever materials you need—notes, visuals, handouts, etc.

SESSION 5

Personal Reflection

Page 170 in the Participant Journal

1. Do you recognize a thread that connects your personal gifts, talents, and passions to what you are hearing God say to you about your purpose?
2. What activities do you find yourself drawn to in order to express your passion?
3. Make a list of creative ways to express the passion in your heart.
4. What is God saying to you about your project?

The *Promise Principle*

Page 174 in the Participant Journal

Read Ephesians 5

1. Underline the promises as you read.
2. Identify the promise as a truth or a commandment.
3. Ask the Holy Spirit what circumstance in your life is touched by this promise.
4. Do you need to ask, do you need to receive it, or both?
5. Pray it!
6. Journal what the Holy Spirit is saying to you.

Now ask yourself:

- What characteristics of God did I discover?
- What does this say about the character of God?

session 6

Session 6

····●···

Leader Coaching Note
Spiritual maturity is the goal of every believer. The more we understand the character and nature of God, the more we will reflect His love for people.

····●···

Agenda

	8–10 Participants (75 Minutes)	11–20 Participants (120 Minutes)
Welcome/Greet/Prayer	5 minutes	5 minutes
Activation: Project Presentations	65 minutes	110 minutes
Homework Explanation & Closing Prayer	5 minutes	5 minutes

Character Builder
CHRISTLIKENESS

Page 179 in the Participant Journal

Definition

- Christ Himself is our righteousness.
- To be Christlike is not to think of ourselves as *like* Him but to be conformed to His image as true disciples (Romans 5:1). In Romans 13:13–14, Paul says to put on the character of the Lord. In Philippians 2:5, he encourages us to have the mind of Christ. And in Galatians 5:16, 22–23, Paul charges us to walk as Christ walked.

  For whom He foreknew, He also predestined to be conformed to the image of His son (Romans 8:29).

Reading

1 Samuel 18:6–16; 19:1; 26:1–25; 27:7–12; Colossians 3:12–16

Biblical Application

- What did Saul's lack of humility cost him?
- Was he a servant leader? Give an example for your answer.

- Name a situation where you read that Saul acted for his own benefit.
- Did he try to bring about unity? Give an example for your answer.
- Name a situation where Saul created contention.

Personal Application

- Compare Saul's leadership with Jesus' leadership.
- Think about Jesus' life:
    - How did He lead with humility? How can you lead with more humility?
    - How did He serve? How can you lead with a servant's heart?
    - How did He act with integrity? What choices do you need to make to lead with greater integrity?
    - How did He work for unity? List situations you face today that require you to contend for unity; define the actions you will take.

Therefore, as God's chosen people, holy and DEARLY LOVED, clothe yourselves with COMPASSION, KINDNESS, HUMILITY, GENTLENESS AND PATIENCE. BEAR WITH EACH OTHER AND FORGIVE ONE ANOTHER if any of you has a grievance against someone. FORGIVE as the Lord FORGAVE YOU. AND OVER ALL THESE VIRTUES PUT ON LOVE, which binds them all together in PERFECT UNITY.

COLOSSIANS 3:12-14 (NIV)

Activation: Project Presentations

Page 183 in the Participant Journal

Leader Coaching Note

This session will be one of the most exciting and revealing of your entire time with the women. Their projects are more than mere homework assignments—they truly reveal a lot about each potential leader's passions, gifts, interests, and strengths. Take notes as the women present their projects. These notes will later help you remember specifics about each participant as you look for volunteers and leaders for your ministry.

Leader Instructions

Set the stage. Today is a celebration of achievement as the women present their projects. Remind the women how far they have come and how much God has done in their hearts. Tell them how proud you are of their hard work and willingness to be vulnerable.

Before the presentations begin, remind everyone of the five-minute time limit. Then tell the women to turn to page 183 in the Participant Journal. Read the Participant Instructions (see below) out loud.

Participant Instructions

Use the space provided to make notes about the various projects presented today. Write down anything that inspires, encourages, or resonates with your heart.

Leader Instructions

Give a one-minute warning to let each speaker know when her time is almost up. Sometimes it is difficult to cut the speaker off because everyone wants to hear her story. If a participant goes over the time limit, ask her to quickly summarize and close.

Homework: Assignment of Your Choice

Page 186 in the Participant Journal

Leader Coaching Note

As we prepare the wrap up of a class, we assign the reading of Chapter 1 in Integrity: The Courage to Meet the Demands of Reality *by Dr. Henry Cloud. We assign this book because it stays with the emphasis on leadership development. This book becomes a focal point for the establishment of small groups we form from the participants who finish the class. You may choose another resource or simply involve the women in your church's existing community structure. We find that the women want a plan to help them continue to meet and encourage each other. Be creative and prayerful as you decide on a plan of action.*

Participant Instructions

- Read Chapter 1 in *Integrity: The Courage to Meet the Demands of Reality* by Dr. Henry Cloud (or another comparable resource of your choice).
- Make a note of your questions and highlight points that stand out to you in the book.

Personal Reflection

Page 189 in the Participant Journal

1. List any additional reflections on your overall WILD experience.
2. What are some personal steps you will commit to taking so you can continue your leadership development journey?

SESSION 6

The *Promise Principle*

Page 191 in the Participant Journal

Read Ephesians 6

1. Underline the promises as you read.
2. Identify the promise as a truth or a commandment.
3. Ask the Holy Spirit what circumstance in your life is touched by this promise.
4. Do you need to ask, do you need to receive it, or both?
5. Pray it!
6. Journal what the Holy Spirit is saying to you.

Now ask yourself:

- What characteristics of God did I discover?
- What does this say about the character of God?

session 7

Session 7

Leader Coaching Note

Understanding the importance, power, and protection of mutual submission to one another is a critical sign of spiritual growth.

Agenda

	8–10 Participants (75 Minutes)	11–20 Participants (120 Minutes)
Welcome/Greet/Prayer	5 minutes	5 minutes
Teaching: Embracing What's Next	20 minutes	30 minutes
Activation: Ongoing Community	35 minutes	70 minutes
Activation: Celebration	5 minutes	5 minutes
Evaluation Forms	5 minutes	5 minutes
Closing Prayer & Blessing	5 minutes	5 minutes

Character Builder
SUBMISSION

Page 197 in the Participant Journal

Definition

- The act of accepting or yielding to a superior or to the will or authority of another

  Rest in the Lord,
  and wait patiently for Him (Psalm 37:7).

Reading

Acts 13:1-3; Philippians 2:5-11; Hebrews 12:1-3; James 1:4

Biblical Application

Thirteen years passed as Paul waited on the Lord to fulfill the promise of the call on his life. Paul submitted his calling to the timing and will of God.

Personal Application

- Find Scripture promises to help you grow in submission as you wait on the promises of God to be fulfilled in your life. Here are some examples:

  "Commit your way to the Lord,
  Trust also in Him,
  And He shall bring *it* to pass" (Psalm 37:5).

  "For they shall not be ashamed who wait for Me" (Isaiah 49:23).

- Make a list of steps you can take to prepare yourself for the call God has spoken to you. Here are some examples:
  - Further my education
  - Develop my speaking and/or writing skills
  - Learn how to practice and master these skills
  - List and rank my skills according to how often I need to work on them
    - Daily
    - Weekly
    - Monthly

SESSION 7

Teaching: Embracing What's Next

Page 200 in the Participant Journal

· • · ● · • ·

Leader Coaching Note
As the women move through WILD, they will naturally want to increase their impact. They will begin to imagine what their destinies and passions might produce. This teaching will help them remain patient with God's timing. After a breakthrough season with God, a period of waiting often follows. This in-between time can either confirm a woman's confidence in God or convince her that she really didn't hear Him.

· • · ● · • ·

Introduction

When we have a spiritual breakthrough like the one we have experienced in WILD, we emerge not only with a vision for the future but also with an expectation about its timing. Almost every believer has periods of time between understanding the call of God on her life and stepping into the new season of obedience. We may feel *ready* to lead but seem stuck on the sidelines while watching others lead. This teaching focuses on how to walk through the upcoming "in-between times" with love, faithfulness, humility, and anticipation of what God has in store for us. The goal of this teaching is to assure you that God is faithful to His Word and His gifts are irrevocable; however, the timing is His alone.

Examples from Scripture

The Bible contains many examples of individuals who had a long season of preparation between their initial understanding of God's plan for their lives and the actual walking out of their destinies.

- **Moses**: God called him at age 40 but did not send him until age 80.
- **Joseph**: He had many years between his dream and his appointment as second-in-command of Egypt.
- **Abraham and Sarah**: They had a 25-year wait between God's promise and the birth of their son, Isaac.
- **Joshua**: He served Moses in the dessert for 40 years before he was appointed as Israel's leader.
- **David**: He was about 17 years old when Samuel anointed him king over Israel. Historians believe David was around 30 years old when he fully took over the royal position.
- **Jesus**: When He acknowledged He was called to His Father's business, He was 12 years old. At age 30, Jesus was baptized and commissioned by God Himself.
- **Paul:** There were 13 years between Paul's Damascus Road experience and when the apostles laid hands on him and sent him out with Barnabas.

While You Are Waiting

While you are waiting for God's promises to happen, you might experience a few trials, seasons of uncertainty, or even what feels like failure or demotion. During this time, ask yourself, "How will I hold onto what God said during my WILD season?" God often uses the in-between time to build character in us so we can withstand spiritual warfare and realize the public impact of our calling. We want God to be the One who determines the timing of our leadership.

SESSION 7

Four Tips to Help You Navigate the In-betweens of Leadership

1. Trust God.

- Hold on to what God has said to you.
- Predetermine the attitude and position of your heart.

Trust in the Lord with all your heart,
And lean not on your own understanding;
In all your ways acknowledge Him, And He shall direct your paths.
(Proverbs 3:5-6)

2. Allow Christ's character to be formed in you.

Therefore, as God's chosen people, holy and dearly loved, clothe yourselves with compassion, kindness, humility, gentleness and patience. Bear with each other and forgive one another if any of you has a grievance against someone. Forgive as the Lord forgave you. And over all these virtues put on love, which binds them all together in perfect unity (Colossians 3:12–14 NIV).

3. Put on the fruit of the Spirit.

- Clothe yourself in the fruit of the Spirit so you may be pleasing to God and a blessing to those around you.
- Review the list in Galatians 2 and select one fruit you want to grow stronger in wearing.

4. Practice.

- Journal or blog. It is crucial to find *your voice* so you are able to communicate well.
- Become confident in delivering your message by using the speaking skills taught in WILD. Consider leading a life group.
- Sharpen your gifts by using them to serve others. You may discover gifts you didn't realize you had.

Summary

God has called you to a purpose and a passion. Prepare yourself by allowing the Holy Spirit to lead you and begin mastering your gifts today. As you wait for the season to come, get ready so you don't miss it. Remember, God is faithful to complete His work.

SESSION 7

Activation: Ongoing Community Involvement

Page 207 in the Participant Journal

· • · · ● · · • ·

Leader Coaching Note

WILD participants enjoy their experience so much that they often ask how they can continue to meet together. Many classes have formed private Facebook pages, met for reunions, or kept in touch by sharing their contact information. You will know what type of follow-up gathering, training, or leadership opportunity is best for the women in your class. At Gateway Church, we continue to nurture the sense of belonging by asking the women to continue gathering in small groups, which we form during this activation. After WILD concludes, be available to answer any questions your small group leader may have and help her follow up with the other members of the class.

· • · · ● · · • ·

Leader Instructions: Before Class

Before Session 7, identify an individual in your class with natural leadership ability and invite her to serve as a small group leader. (If you have a large class, you may wish to have multiple small group leaders). Coach this individual on your expectations and goals. She will select a book for the small group to study. (At Gateway Church, we use *Integrity: The Courage to Meet the Demands of Reality* by Dr. Henry Cloud.) The small group leader will facilitate this activation as a practice for leading the small group.

Leader Instructions: During Class

- Ask the women to divide into two or more discussion groups, depending on the size of the class.

- Introduce the small group leader and allow her to lead the remainder of the activation.
    - If you have multiple small group leaders, have each one lead a discussion group.

Small Group Leader Instructions
- Briefly introduce the book study of your choice. Explain why you've chosen this particular book, give a topical introduction, and share how it will help the women in their continuing spiritual development.
- Formally invite the women to continue gathering with their discussion group outside of WILD.
    - Ask for a volunteer in each group to host in her home.
    - Get contact information from each person in the small group.
    - If possible, schedule the first small group meeting.

SESSION 7

Activation: Celebration!

Page 210 in the Participant Journal

· · · • · · • · ·

Leader Coaching Note

Congratulations! You've reached the final exercise of your WILD class. You and your participants will enjoy taking a few moments to celebrate all God has done. Take time to pray over the women and thank them for trusting you and participating in the class. Communicate your love for them and your heart for their future.

· · · • · · • · ·

Leader Instructions

Read the Participant Instructions (see below) out loud. If time permits, ask for volunteers to share their answers.

Participant Instructions

Thinking about your entire WILD experience, what was …

1. Your favorite teaching?
2. The most impactful moment?
3. The biggest surprise?

Until We Meet Again

Page 211 in the Participant Journal

· • · • ● • · • ·

Leader Coaching Note
Feedback is essential to help you build upon and improve each WILD class. You can make photocopies of the sample evaluation form provided in the Getting Started section of this Leader Guide, or you are welcome to create your own. Bring enough copies for each participant to have one.

· • · • ● • · • ·

Leader Instructions
Read the Participant Instructions (see below) out loud.

Participant Instructions
One of our primary goals is to ensure you continue to experience a sense of belonging and fellowship with your fellow WILD participants. We highly encourage you to build on these new relationships by meeting with your small group and volunteering in your area of interest.

Your feedback is so important and helpful because it allows us to continue to improve the WILD experience for others. You will receive an evaluation form from your leader. Please complete it and return it to your leader before leaving.

Thank you for participating in WILD and sharing your heart with us. May God bless you as you continue on your leadership journey.

Leader Instructions

Pass out the evaluation forms. Encourage the women to be open and honest—their feedback really does matter! Be sure to collect the forms before the women leave.

About Gateway Women

Gateway Women is led by Debbie Morris. She is the visionary leader behind Pink Impact and serves as the executive pastor of Gateway Women at Gateway Church. She is the author of *The Blessed Woman*, and coauthor of *The Blessed Marriage* and *Living Right Side Up*. She's a quiet but powerful influence in the lives of the women at Gateway Church as well as the Christian community. Debbie's heart is to help women understand who they are in God, discover their destinies, and experience victory in life. As a wife who witnessed God turn her marriage around, she delights in encouraging women to believe that God can and will do the same for them. Debbie is married to Pastor Robert Morris, her high school sweetheart and founding senior pastor of Gateway Church. They have been married for 36 years and have three married children and eight grandchildren.

About Pink Impact

Founded in 2006, Pink Impact is Gateway Church's annual conference for women. Pink Impact is renowned for providing women an opportunity to participate in an environment that exposes them to the goodness of God, invites them to join in His kingdom work, and saturates them in an empowering culture that celebrates women. Each year, thousands of women from around the world gather to engage in extravagant worship, be inspired by gifted communicators, and build new friendships.

pinkimpact.com

Additional Gateway Women Resources

The Blessed Woman
Debbie Morris

Living Rightside Up
Debbie Morris and Friends

The Blessed Marriage
Debbie Morris

Women at War
Jan Greenwood

Make Your Mark: A 40-Day Devotional from Gateway Women

Gateway Worship Voices: Women of Gateway

Resources are available at store.gatewaypeople.com and Amazon.com.

THE PROMISE PRINCIPLE
A New Way to Encounter the Bible

Phillip Hunter

The apostle Peter says, *"Make every effort to respond to God's promises"* (2 Peter 1:5).

God's Word is full of promises, but we often miss them. Circumstances may shape how you read the Bible; however, the Bible should shape how you respond to your circumstances. Learning to recognize God's promises leads to spiritual growth. The Promise Principle teaches you how to discover these promises. This is not a Bible study but a fresh way to read the Word. It has the power to change the way you face every circumstance in your life.

This technique is:
- Simple and practical—anyone can do it!
- Personal and relevant
- For use by individuals or groups
- A discipleship tool for leaders

Phillip Hunter has a master of divinity and has spent two decades in full-time ministry with camps, parachurch organizations, and churches. He currently serves as an executive pastor at Gateway Church in the Dallas/Fort Worth Metroplex. Phillip's passion is to see people transformed by Christ, growing in spiritual maturity, and living as God saved them to be. Phillip Hunter began the *Promise Principle™* journey fifteen years ago and has shared this life-changing technique with youth and adults across the United States and throughout the world.

Book ISBN: 9781945529146
Journal ISBN: 9781945529160

You can find **The Promise Principle** and the companion journal at the Gateway Bookstore and wherever Christian books are sold. **The Promise Principle** is also available as an eBook and audiobook.

GATEWAY PUBLISHING